HISTORIC PHOTOS OF
SAN FRANCISCO CRIME

TEXT AND CAPTIONS BY HANNAH CLAYBORN

TURNER
PUBLISHING COMPANY

Members of the San Francisco Police Department strut their stuff during the annual review of 1900. The San Francisco Police Department had much to be proud of. By the turn of the century, San Franciscans felt safe in their city, assured that vigilante raids and hoodlum riots were things of the past. Yet while Police Chief William P. Sullivan was warning his force to stop wasting duty time dyeing their hair and whiskers, girls as young as 14 were being fed into sordid cribs and brothels, and hapless sailors were still being fleeced and "shanghaied" regularly at dance halls and waterfront dives. Opium use was rampant not only in Chinatown, but also in a growing number of white middle-class homes. Some would soon call the police department "rotten to the core."

HISTORIC PHOTOS OF
SAN FRANCISCO CRIME

Turner Publishing Company
200 4th Avenue North • Suite 950
Nashville, Tennessee 37219
(615) 255-2665

www.turnerpublishing.com

Historic Photos of San Francisco Crime

Library of Congress Control Number: 2009922656

ISBN: 978-1-59652-534-4

Printed in China

09 10 11 12 13 14 15 16—0 9 8 7 6 5 4 3 2 1

Contents

Two bound prisoners wait with an official at the iron gate of San Quentin's dungeon, built in the mid-1850s and used for solitary confinement punishment for 80 years. Originally intended to house 45 prisoners, the dungeon may be California's oldest surviving public work, built out of local rock and brick quarried by convicts. Because of the date and the unusual pairing of the inmates shown here, these prisoners may be Louis Dabner and John Seimson, known as the "Gas Pipe Thugs," responsible for four murders and several assaults and robberies between August and November of 1906. Seimson was a full-blood Hawaiian, 28 at the time of his execution. Dabner, who listed his occupation as "playboy," was 16 when arrested and 18 when executed. According to author William J. Duffy, their execution by hanging at San Quentin on July 31, 1908, drew record crowds as the first double execution in state history.

ACKNOWLEDGMENTS

This volume, *Historic Photos of San Francisco Crime,* is the result of the cooperation and effort of many individuals, organizations, and corporations. It is with great thanks that we acknowledge the valuable contribution of the following for their generous support:

The Bancroft Library, University of California, Berkeley
The California History Room, California State Library, Sacramento, California
Library of Congress
Novato History Museum
San Francisco History Center, San Francisco Public Library
The Virtual Museum of the City of San Francisco, www.sfmuseum.org

This book is dedicated to the legion of "pretty waiter girls" who were forced to make a living for themselves in one of the most heartless and depraved places on earth, the Old Barbary Coast in San Francisco.

This book is also dedicated to Jesse B. Cook (1860–1938), Officer, Chief of Police, and Police Commissioner serving the San Francisco Police Department from the late 1880s to the 1930s. His intelligence and sympathy for unfortunates, even criminals, was evident. He was an honest cop in an era when many were not, and his love of the police department, San Francisco, and California history led him to record and collect much of the information and many of the images in this book.

With the exception of touching up imperfections that have accrued with the passage of time and cropping where necessary, no changes have been made to the photographs. The focus and clarity of many photographs is limited by the technology and the ability of the photographer at the time they were taken.

PREFACE

The crimes of San Francisco's early history—the hotheaded lynchings, Committee of Vigilance uprisings, and the exploits of Black Bart—tend to overshadow the half century of fascinating crime that followed, which is the subject of this book. Some early dens of iniquity, gambling parlors, saloons, and dance halls of the Barbary Coast remained constant in both eras, even resurrecting themselves after a cataclysmic earthquake and fire in 1906. They would thrive until the illicit activities that sustained them—robbery, prostitution, and gambling—were driven farther underground in 1917.

The "Hoodlums" of San Francisco's waterfront and the tongs of Chinatown were notable criminal consortiums of the nineteenth century, two cultural sides of one coin minted on the violent streets of San Francisco in the late 1860s. A reporter for the *San Francisco Times* in the 1860s offered this explanation of the term "Hoodlum" to the readers of the *Los Angeles Express* on August 25, 1877:

> *A gang of bad boys from fourteen to nineteen years of age were associated for the purpose of stealing. These boys had a rendezvous, and when danger threatened them their words of warning were, 'Huddle 'em! Huddle 'em!' An article headed "Huddle 'Em," describing the gang and their plans of operation, was published in the* San Francisco Times. *The name applied to them was soon contracted to hoodlum.*

According to author Herbert Asbury, an eyewitness claimed that "huddle 'em" was not a warning cry, but a cue for gang action to surround a likely victim for mauling and robbery. By 1868, these boys, along with an occasional girl, operated from an abandoned shack on an old wharf with an entrance underneath, and were already credited with scores of robberies. Over a generation, as younger boys followed their lead, the Hoodlums became something of an institution. One defining feature of the Hoodlum was his uniform hatred of the Chinese, an indication that his background was working-class Irish. Hoodlums made belts and cap tassels out of queues they cut from the heads of Chinese men, beat and mutilated them for no particular reason, and set fire to their washhouses and shops. This pastime climaxed in the riot of July 24, 1877, when several hundred hoodlums burned and wrecked Chinese businesses, attacking every Chinese immigrant unlucky enough to cross their path.

Some authors claim that there was a model in China for the violent San Francisco tongs, a word that simply means association. Others think the tongs were as American as chop suey. The mother of all American tongs, the Chee Kung tong, originally accepted all those who could not join the existing Chinese benevolent associations that were based on family name or birthplace. The Chee Kung, therefore, was an association of disenfranchised young men, much like the Irish street urchins, who first banded together for protection, but soon mimicked the violence, robbery, and extortion that surrounded them. Each group filtered that violence through its own cultural traditions.

The feared "hatchet men" or "highbinders" of Chinatown were hired killers who first concealed their weapons in fabric wound high about their waists. In those early days they left a sharpened lather's cleaver in the skull of their victim, but later adopted modern weapons. While Hoodlums as a specific group dissipated in one generation, the tongs increased in number and power. According to a February 13, 1886, account in *Harper's Weekly,* the Chee Kung tong had 4,500 members in San Francisco, and 15,000 throughout America in 390 branches. They enjoyed luxurious headquarters in a three-story building on Spofford Alley. Law-abiding Chinese could not resist the demands of such a powerful organization, able to seek them out wherever they might flee. By the turn of the century, there were at least 30 tongs directing their violence largely upon each other while competing for gambling, opium, and prostitution (slave girl) revenue.

According to San Francisco Police Department Commissioner Jesse B. Cook, one of the most famous tong kingpins of the nineteenth century, "Little Pete," copied his extortion techniques from the Hoodlums who periodically raided Chinatown, demanding tribute money from storeowners. Born Fung Jing Toy in China around 1864, Little Pete immigrated to the United States with his family at the age of five. Watching, learning, and probably suffering from the worst of the Hoodlum raids in his youth, Little Pete ascended the ladder of the tong underworld swiftly. As a young man in his twenties, he stalked the streets of Chinatown wearing a steel-reinforced hat and chain mail, and was considered invincible until murdered by a rival in 1897. That execution lit the fuse of the twentieth-century tong wars.

And what became of the Hoodlums, those beastie boys of the Barbary Coast who disappeared from the headlines in the mid-1890s? If they survived their youth, they would likely have ended up in one of two places depending on their choices and character: San Quentin Prison or the San Francisco Police Department, which was, without a doubt, the toughest gang in town. As the curtain rose on the new century, the scene was a different tale of two cities, San Francisco and within it the impenetrable cultural kernel of Chinatown, the only neighborhood not ruled by the SFPD.

—*Hannah Clayborn*

The Cobweb Palace was a saloon built by Abraham Warner in 1856 on the northwest corner of Meigg's Wharf and Francisco Street (now Fisherman's Wharf). Unlike Barbary Coast criminal hangouts such as the Cowboy's Rest and the Whale on Pacific Street, this North Beach survivor catered to respectable old salts with heavy pockets and time to kill. The Cobweb Palace's shiplap siding and lack of pretense were entirely typical of the dives, nickel dance halls, and "bagnios" (brothels) that flourished for over 60 years on the Barbary Coast, an area that spread from its original nucleus at the foot of Broadway and Pacific streets.

A BARBARY COAST HANGOVER

(1890–1909)

By the first decade of the twentieth century, bars, dance halls, and brothels filled the Barbary Coast and North Beach and had infiltrated the Tenderloin, serving as headquarters for gambling, drugs, and prostitution. Prominent citizens held open interests in this shadow economy as landlords or regulators ripe for bribery.

Attorney Abraham Ruef had extensive gambling interests when he picked Eugene Schmitz to mold into the perfect mayoral candidate for his Union Labor Party. Soon after Schmitz was elected in 1901, Ruef initiated an unprecedented spree of bribery, graft, and influence peddling. But Ruef blundered in 1903 when he approached sugar magnate Rudolph Spreckels with a profiteering scheme involving a manufactured streetcar strike and the sale of municipal bonds. Instead, Spreckels joined forces with newspaper editor Fremont Older to campaign against Schmitz and "Boss" Ruef, and enlisted the aid of President Theodore Roosevelt, who sent federal prosecutors to investigate.

In the wake of the earthquake and fire of 1906, a crime wave made San Franciscans afraid to step outside their doors, as bank robbers and murderers struck in broad daylight. Several men died in violent street fighting that erupted between labor unions and police during the Streetcar Strikes of 1906 and 1907, which may have been instigated by Ruef.

The Oliver Grand Jury eventually indicted 40 civil servants for 175 crimes, and an official report described the police department as "rotten to the core." Supervisors had accepted bribes from most public utilities and United Railroads. Abe Ruef's network made a last desperate attempt to save itself during the second corruption trial in 1907. SFPD detectives allied with United Railroads, kidnapped Fremont Older, ostensibly on a libel charge, and tried to take him to Los Angeles. While Older was rescued unharmed, rumors circulated that the detectives intended to shoot him during an "escape attempt." Then on April 29, 1908, the home of chairman of the board of supervisors, James L. Gallagher, was bombed. Although the family escaped injury, part of their home was wrecked. The bomber had been hired by a United Railroads employee. Soon after, a Ruef operative walked up to prosecutor Francis J. Heney in his own courtroom and shot him in the head. Heney survived, but the gunman was found murdered in his jail cell the next morning. Finally, the newly appointed police chief, William Biggy, disappeared from his patrol boat in the dead of night on November 30, 1908, his body washing up on the rocks of Angel Island two weeks later.

Most saloons and dance halls had "pretty waiter girls" who often moonlighted as prostitutes in "cow yards" out back, or in upstairs rooms. Although the Cobweb Palace was infested with many more spiders than criminals, Abraham Warner, pictured here around 1895, was no saint. He loved paintings of naked women as much as he loved arachnids, and his lusty Louvre exceeded a thousand paintings, barely visible beneath the dust. The Cobweb Palace also featured exotic birds and animals in cages. According to author Herbert Asbury, one of Warner's parrots had a severe drinking problem and, when soused, could curse in four languages.

The city's first prison was actually a ship, the brig *Euphemia*, purchased by the city council in 1849 for $3,500. Frequent escapes from its hold contributed to citizen outrage that led to the formation of the first Committee of Vigilance. The next jail site was the Graham House City Hall at Pacific and Montgomery streets, then the basement of the former Jenny Lind Theater at Washington and Kearny streets, converted to a city hall in 1852. This view shows the city prison in the basement of the City Hall at McAllister and Larkin streets in 1895.

Ignatius Pierce should have had a good
life. The son of a prominent and wealthy
retired sea captain, Nelson Pierce, and
Antonia Cruz, member an old Mexican
family, Ignatius was born on Greenwich
Street in North Beach. Whether the
neighborhood hoodlums, alcohol, or
discrimination against Mexicans played a
role, both Ignatius and his brother, Nelson
Junior, spent most of their unhappy lives
in jail for robbery and burglary. Ignatius
was finally remanded to San Quentin for
25 years for murdering John Peterson, a
night watchman at the Richmond House.
He died in prison in 1891.

James Egan was a homeboy, one of many whose memory is reduced to a few sad notes beneath a police mug shot. Alcohol may have played a role in his downfall. Born on Russell Street between Hyde and Larkin, James attended Spring Valley School on Broadway. Census records show he was the second of three children born to Irish immigrants, and his father, William, became a local saloonkeeper. James became a "desperate" young man who spent a great deal of time in jail. He may have joined the hoodlum element that emerged in the city in the late 1860s. On September 8, 1888, James was convicted for murdering a man in a saloon brawl at Bay and Larkin streets and was sentenced to 35 years at San Quentin. Finally making parole after serving 21 years, he died soon after, just one of many casualties of the Barbary Coast.

Many streetwalkers moonlighted profitably as pickpockets. Police might turn a blind eye to harlotry or shanghaied sailors, but not to the robbery of citizens—if they were brave enough to report it. Jesse B. Cook's police scrapbook wistfully memorializes Mabel Keating, seen here in 1895, as a "clever pickpocket" and a "fine looking woman" who roamed Dupont Street (now Grant Avenue) in Old Chinatown, preying on male tourists staying at the big hotels. These girls specialized in fleecing their Johns as they lay in a drunken stupor, or by having accomplices assault their customers. Mabel left for Chicago around 1895, probably to work the upcoming World's Fair.

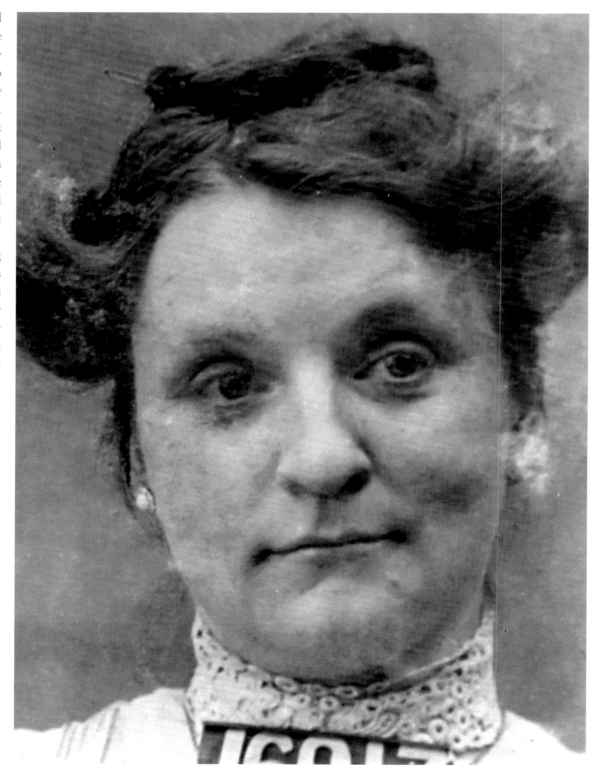

This young prostitute and pickpocket, Mary Plaza, came from the Italian quarter east of Russian Hill. Like so many others, she counted on her Johns to suffer in silence rather than broadcast their debauchery by pressing charges. She miscalculated with a man named Frank Godence, who prosecuted her for theft. She jumped bail in December 1905, soon after this photograph was taken, and was never heard from again.

Arnold Genthe, a famous photographer who captured many images of Chinatown between 1896 and 1906, recorded this image of himself inspecting his camera on a Chinatown sidewalk. Almost certainly staged, it carried the title "An Unsuspecting Victim," an obvious allusion to the dangers posed by pickpockets in Chinatown. In at least one published version, Genthe doctored the image, erasing the Caucasian man with the beard, making it appear that the danger emanated from the Chinese man walking past on the sidewalk behind him. In reality, the Chinese man was observing two Caucasians acting in a typically inscrutable manner.

Although looks can be deceiving, there is much about this 1905 photograph of pickpocket and probable prostitute May Kirby that rends the heart. The sullen defiance of her features cannot obscure her obvious youth, and her carefully elevated coiffure, tied with a schoolgirl's bow, gives the impression that she is relatively new to the underworld of the Barbary Coast. Girls as young as 14 or 15 roamed the streets of San Francisco. According to Jesse B. Cook, May Kirby's beat was Chinatown, where she found wealthy tourists in the labyrinthine alleyways. She was last seen just before the earthquake and fire of 1906.

Prostitute and pickpocket Annie Green, seen here around 1900, also counted on her customers not to prosecute and thereby admit to a liaison with a prostitute, especially with a black woman. Some women worked at dives that specialized in drugging drinks of unsuspecting customers with laudanum, a form of opium, to make them more malleable.

Author Herbert Asbury called the Chinese gambler "the most persistent and reckless gamester on earth." Retired Chief of Police Jesse B. Cook claimed that men confined to 12 blocks in Chinatown had little else to amuse them. In the 1890s, Cook estimated that 62 lottery agents, 50 fan tan games, and 8 lottery drawings operated in Chinatown. A Chinatown Squad had been formed in 1886 to control vice, but authorities generally tolerated gambling throughout the city until 1914. During earlier attempts to purge corrupt members of the police department, Chinatown Squad leader Thomas Ellis was dismissed for incompetence and bribery in 1904 for failure to control gambling, and his boss, acting Chief of Police Captain George Wittman, was dismissed in 1905.

Opium was originally used as a medicine, and although the Chinese Imperial Court tried to ban its use and importation in the early 1800s, it was a common recreational drug in China by 1849. Opium came with the first immigrants to Chinatown, and some Chinese merchants became wealthy importing shipments of up to 2,000 pounds. Forced into an overcrowded ghetto and lacking the support of families, single Chinese men often found solace in the opium pipe. Like those using many other drugs, some opium users could control their intake, while others became hopeless addicts. This opium addict was photographed by Arnold Genthe in Chinatown around 1900.

Although Westerners used opiates in a liquid form known as laudanum or paragoric, opium smoking was viewed with a mixture of disgust and fascination by most Caucasians. Opium den tours became so popular that they were enlivened with actors fabricating events. Using routes that led from one cellar to another, clever guides created the impression of penetrating into networks of tunnels deep underground. Thrilling incidents involving "hatchet men" were often staged. This den was allegedly photographed by flashlight, surprising the occupants (ca. 1900).

This "slave girl" looks through a small window in the door of her crib around 1900. Trafficking in human flesh was a tragic reality in Chinatown half a century after the Emancipation Proclamation took effect. Windows like these allowed potential customers to select and pimps to supervise these enslaved prostitutes. This girl would be required to solicit men by calling through the window when she was not otherwise occupied. Usually initiated into the cribs and "cow yards" by the age of 14, so hard and dangerous were their lives that Chinese slave girls over 20 years old were a rarity.

Several missions formed over the years to convert and help abandoned, enslaved, or abused children of Chinatown. Old St. Mary's Presbyterian Church, the first Asian church in North America, was built in Chinatown in 1853. The Presbyterian Mission Home for Chinese Women opened in 1874. The Chinese Congregational Church and Chinese United Methodist Church were established in Chinatown in 1873, and the Salvation Army came in 1886. Although the missions refused enlightened medical procedures to stop the spread of sexually transmitted diseases, their combined work saved thousands of girls and orphans from domestic slavery and prostitution. Yet no individual is remembered with more reverence than Donaldina Cameron, who came to the Presbyterian Mission Home in 1895 to teach Asian women sewing, but stayed her entire life, saving over 3,000 women and children during her 47 years there. The mission, now known as the Donaldina Cameron House, is still active in Chinatown.

A tong boss strides down a Chinatown street with his wary bodyguard following behind (ca. 1900). Gambling, prostitution, and other profitable vices like contract murder were eventually taken over by tongs, a word that simply means association or lodge. As early as 1860, the first recorded incidence of a tong war took place in the gold camps of Marysville, where a fight over a woman escalated into a battle between the Hop Sings (the Hall of Associated Conquerors) and the Suey Sings (the Hall of Auspicious Victory). Tongs multiplied and spread throughout the West, but nowhere were they more numerous than in San Francisco's Chinatown, where by the 1890s it is estimated that up to 30 different groups vied for control.

As the new century began, old tong feuds simmered. Only three years before, a major tong boss, Fung Jing Toy ("Little Pete") had been murdered in a barbershop, setting off a series of reprisals that continued for months. When it wanted to fight, a tong would issue a written proclamation to a rival, a challenge posted on walls in several locations around Chinatown. Residents would nervously watch for these proclamations and their posted responses just before open street fighting broke out. Also posted were notices of those trying to get free of a tong, warning hatchet men that their tong would not pay for their murder since they had defected. This wall was photographed around 1900.

According to author Richard H. Dillon, by the 1890s, the Bing Kong, Wah Ting San Fong, and On Yik tongs had taken over brothels; Kwong Duck and On Leong tongs handled the slave girls for those brothels; and the Hip Sing tong controlled gambling in Chinatown. Wong Fook, one of Chinatown's "Big Eight" tong bosses, is seen here in 1898 flanked by Mary Lee (left) and Susie (or Ossie) Wong. The remaining seven of the "Big Eight" were Chang Chung, Buck Guy, Jim Wong, Wong You, Chin Chow, Chin Kim You, Quong Bing (alias Chop Wollar), and Wong Wo King.

The Chinatown Squad was established in the early 1880s. By 1889, a young police officer named Jesse B. Cook headed up the squad before he went on to serve as chief of police and then police commissioner. Chinatown Squad members in 1905 were, from left to right, Officer T. O'Connell, Officer Fred Krack, Officer H. Bolton, and Officer Ed. Casey in the back row; Lieutenant Collins, Officer Ed Foley, Officer O. Burg, Officer R. Curtin, and Officer T. Hanley in the second row; unidentified, Officer T. Curtis, Officer T. Conley, Lieutenant Cliff Fields, and Lieutenant Dan Cronin in the third row; and Sergeant William Ross and Corporal William Ferguson in the front row.

Although it was a cataclysm of biblical proportions for San Francisco, the earthquake and fire that began on the morning of April 18, 1906, was actually a reprieve for Mayor Eugene Schmitz and his manager Abe Ruef. Both men were under investigation for bribery and graft by federal prosecutor Francis J. Heney. On the day of the disaster, as National Guard, police, and fire crews scrambled to control the mayhem, the mayor appointed a Committee of Fifty to help manage the crisis. In this view, taken on the morning of April 18 from the corner of Market and Third streets, two members of the National Guard can be seen conferring as the fire approaches. The Call Building is at far-left and the Examiner Building at far-right.

National Guard troops patrol at Stockton and Ellis streets as the fire rages on April 18, 1906. Flames will soon engulf the Call Building (at center) along with 4.7 square miles of the heart of the city. Mayor Schmitz, working temporarily from the Hall of Justice as the City Hall and jail lay in ruins, ordered the release of all petty offenders. Reports soon arrived that thieves were burglarizing stores and homes, and that the body of a woman was found in the Mission District with her fingers amputated for her rings. Hoodlums were stealing the liquor from saloons. Forthwith, Schmitz issued a proclamation authorizing military and civilian authorities to "KILL any and all persons found engaged in Looting or in the Commission of Any Other Crimes."

A bewildered and frightened crowd watches the flames spread on Grant Avenue on April 18, 1906. The regular police force was augmented by the National Guard, troops from Fort Baker and the Presidio, and "Citizen Patrols." A looter caught while allegedly burglarizing Shreve's Jewelry store at Post Street and Grant Avenue was turned over to a soldier, who immediately killed him and left his body to be consumed by the oncoming fire. Two other unarmed, prominent citizens were among those shot in the days that followed. The city's Superintendent of Children's Playgrounds, Joseph Meyers, was killed by a National Guardsman on April 19. Heber Tilden, returning from his San Mateo home to continue his tireless work for the Red Cross, was shot by a volunteer policeman on April 22.

On April 20, a man who was never identified, seen lying on the sidewalk, was shot by the son of a prominent businessman. Ernest Denicke, a retired National Guardsman, had donned his old uniform, stationing himself near the waterfront, where he came upon a man carrying chickens. Suspecting that he had stolen them, Denicke tried to conscript the man to fight the fire, then ordered a sailor to prod him with a bayonet even after the man had dropped the chickens and tried to leave. Denicke shot the retreating man and later that night weighted the body with iron and had it thrown into the bay. The dead man had probably picked up chickens that had been released from a nearby railway car that stood in the path of the fire. So great was the outrage over the incident that Denicke was indicted twice. But with Boss Abe Ruef and ex-governor James Budd engaged for his defense, the charges against Denicke were dismissed, and he was found not guilty.

With the Hall of Justice at Kearny and Washington streets in the obvious path of the fire, valuable police records were moved across the street to Portsmouth Square, and two detectives were left to guard them. The detectives were given food but no water, a precious commodity throughout the city because of the broken water mains. When tremendous heat and ash threatened to ignite the canvas covering the records, the resourceful officers raided a saloon across the street. For the next 24 hours the canvas was kept moist with bottled beer, and the records as well as the detectives survived the ordeal. This photograph shows the Hall of Justice after the fire had passed.

The National Guard lines up in front of the ruined Hall of Justice across from Portsmouth Square soon after the earthquake in 1906. Despite the confusion and confluence of efforts by firemen, police, military troops, National Guard, and unpredictable citizen volunteers, countless heroic deeds were performed in those first chaotic days. Exhausted men, unsure of the fate of their own families, stayed on duty to help others. The fire chief died when a chimney from a neighboring hotel fell on the station house, and several police officers gave their lives trying to save citizens. Officer Joseph Connelly stayed on duty believing that his family had perished, only to find them one week later in the city of Vallejo.

On the first day of the disaster, the City Hall was ruined and the Hall of Justice, shown here, was swept by fire. Mayor Schmitz ordered prisoners charged with serious crimes transferred to San Quentin, and he released all petty offenders. After the mayor's initial command to shoot all transgressors, instructions were issued to draft all "idle and dissolute" men to assist in clearing the streets, an order that may have been unevenly enforced at best.

During the height of the conflagration, Officer Edward Leonard and Deputy L. K. Jones bravely rushed into the city tax collector's office in the ruined City Hall. They were able to retrieve records that enabled tax collector J. F. Nichols to bring in over $1 million in taxes that year. Much of the city's tax revenue went up in smoke along with the 4.7 square miles of destruction in the heart of downtown.

With cloth sacks slung blithely over their shoulders, police officials remove the coin from the treasury in City Hall, severely damaged by the 1906 earthquake.

Following the earthquake and fire in 1906, hoodlums and thieves intending to trespass on the Hall of Justice ruins (seen in the background) would have to deal with these tough customers. Joining members of the police force in this lineup, charmingly staged for a newspaper photo, are judges Thomas Graham and Frank Kerrigan, marked by Xs at their feet.

This desolate view looks southeast from Stockton and Sacramento streets. The square building at center-left is noted as "an old Chinese Temple." The Chinese survivors of the earthquake were the only group segregated in the refugee camps by nationality. They were forcibly removed from the city and sequestered at the windswept parade grounds above Fort Point. Even after other civilians were allowed into the downtown region, the Chinese were kept out. Meanwhile, wholesale looting by whites, including respectable middle-class women and members of the National Guard, proceeded until at least April 30, before any Chinese were allowed back into Chinatown.

Refugees were housed in one of 12 camps around the city. Here, Sergeant Sills stands outside his headquarters at the Point Lobos refugee camp on Lobos Square, bordered by Octavia, Pacific, Laguna, and Union streets.

FOOD & HOUSE ACCOMODATIONS
FOR 200 PEOPLE AT PT. RICHMOND
Will provide for 1000 if necessary !!!

GROCERIES, WINES & DELICACIES

NO PASSES
REQUIRED through Lines
NO MORE WILL BE issued
J.F. DINAN CHIEF OF POLICE

POLICE STATION.

FINE SA

DELICATE

At 2 P.M., nine hours after the earthquake hit on April 18, 1906, police headquarters moved across the street to Portsmouth Square. Two hours later, it relocated to the Fairmont Hotel, from which it departed the next day as the fire reached and consumed Nob Hill. Alighting momentarily at the North End Station at 1712 Washington Street, it transferred on the afternoon of April 19 to Franklin Hall on Fillmore Street. Two days later it moved to the southwest corner of Bush and Fillmore streets (shown in the photo above with the damaged steeple of St. Dominic's Church in the background), where they remained for several weeks before moving to Lowell High School on Sutter Street, near Gough. Just before school opened, the Board of Education provided a temporary building on a school lot at the southwest corner of Pine and Larkin streets, where it remained until February 11, 1907.

Loss of tax revenue led to cuts in the police department, and criminals quickly took advantage. Banks and shops were held up in broad daylight. Louis Dabner and John Seimson, known as the "Gas Pipe Thugs" for a weapon used in one crime, were responsible for four murders and various robberies and assaults between August and November of 1906. One victim survived the attack, capturing Dabner and later identifying the pair, who were eventually convicted and sentenced to death. From left to right above are Judge E. Shortal, Officer Jack Attridge, unidentified officer, Officer J. Doyle, Captain Thomas Duke, John Seimson, Louis Dabner, and Officer J. Rice.

A French police officer, Alphonse Bertillon, turned his lifelong interest in anthropology into a new science. Bertillon came up with a complex system of criminal identification through measurement and permanent marks, like scars or tattoos, that he named anthropometry. Using it to identify 241 repeat offenders in 1884, the Bertillon System, as it became known, spread quickly to Britain and America. Bertillon also developed a better mug shot and modern crime scene photography. In this view from around 1906, members of the SFPD learn about the system that would soon be used to identify many criminals in San Francisco before it was supplanted by fingerprinting.

Mayor Eugene Schmitz (with beard) drives the first trolley car to run in San Francisco following the earthquake and fire. Schmitz, elected in 1902 as the first Union Labor Party mayor in the United States, was already under investigation for corruption when the earthquake intervened. That investigation would soon resume with devastating results for the mayor. The streetcar workers shown here, known as Carmen, helped elect Mayor Schmitz and were members of one of the most militant of San Francisco's labor unions. They struck in five of the six years from 1902 to 1907, finally leading to the violent Streetcar Strike that erupted on Bloody Tuesday, May 7, 1907. The Streetcar Strike of 1907 had deep roots in the dissatisfaction of the working class and its antipathy toward owners of large companies and corporations, known as Monopolists, or Capitalists.

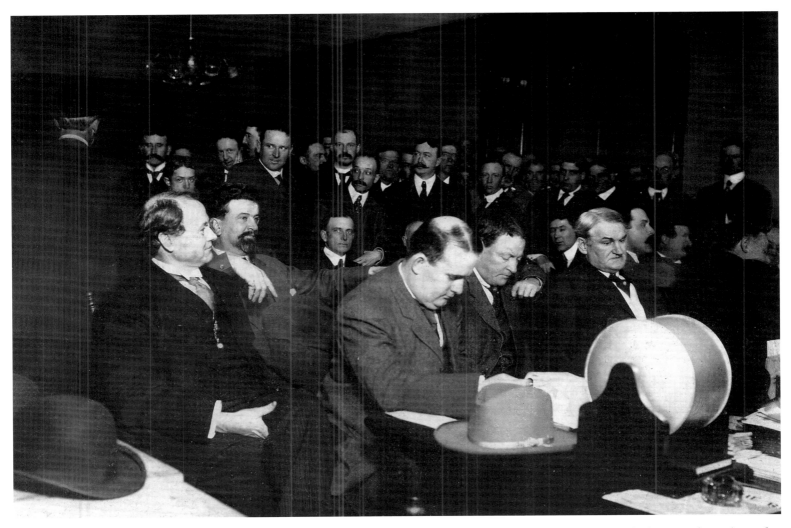

Mayor Eugene Schmitz, seen here in second row with beard at his corruption trial in 1907, was molded by Abraham Ruef into the perfect candidate to lead his Union Labor Party. Ruef went to work soon after Schmitz was elected in 1901, advancing his personal interests and agenda through bribery, graft, and influence peddling. Ruef made a huge blunder in 1903 when he tried to enlist sugar magnate and president of the First National Bank, Rudolph Spreckels, in one of his schemes. Appalled, Spreckels joined forces with Fremont Older, editor of the *News-Call Bulletin,* who ran a campaign against the pair for many months before the 1905 election. Spreckels also enlisted the aid of President Theodore Roosevelt, who assigned federal prosecutor Francis J. Heney and Detective William J. Burns to execute indictments.

The Abraham Ruef–Mayor Eugene Schmitz political machine began to experience mechanical problems in 1906. New District Attorney William H. Langdon decided to revive the long comatose ordinance on vice by ordering raids on many gambling establishments in cigar stores and saloons, where many prominent citizens, including Ruef, had open interests. Slot machines were licensed by city supervisors, bringing Ruef and other saloon and cigar storeowners huge profits. Langdon was not successful, but Ruef and Schmitz would soon be indicted for extortion and bribery involving whiskey, gambling, and prostitution. Shown here in 1899 at the Coronado Bar at the northwest corner of Ellis and Powell streets are (left to right) Abe Ruef, William Cook, Ben Adler, owner of this cigar store, Jesse B. Greenfield, unidentified, and Ed Schafer. Later Ruef would be indicted for his professional connection to the Hilbert Brothers, wholesale whiskey merchants and proprietors of this bar.

In the back seat, from left to right, are Abe Ruef, Detective William Burns, and newly appointed Chief of Police William J. Biggy, who succeeded disgraced Chief Jeremiah F. Dinan, also caught up in the graft trials. During Ruef's second corruption trial, they are arriving at a temporary court facility, the Salvation Army Hall at Fillmore and Post streets, set up after the Hall of Justice was destroyed. Abraham Ruef was born into a prosperous Jewish family and was a brilliant scholar, graduating from UC Berkeley and Hastings Law School. He was admitted to the bar at age 21. As a young man, Ruef was an idealist who helped form the Municipal Reform League to fight corruption. Soon, however, he became a brilliant student prince of the Machiavellian political patronage system in San Francisco, and although he avoided violence, by 1906 had extended his influence by graft and bribery into almost every facet of city government.

As Abe Ruef listens to one of his attorneys, Henry Ach, Police Chief William J. Biggy looks on at far-left during Ruef's second graft trial in 1907. At this trial Ruef tried to bribe a juror through an intermediary, who was later convicted. Ruef also succeeded in getting ex-con saloonkeeper Morris Haas on the jury list. Prosecutor Heney exposed Haas's record as a forger and an adulterer, and Haas was dismissed from the jury. Many weeks later on November 13, 1908, Haas walked up to Heney in the courtroom and shot him in the head. Miraculously, Heney survived the attack with the loss of hearing in one ear. Haas was found shot to death in his jail cell with a derringer in his shoe the next morning—before he could be interrogated. Throughout the Ruef-Schmitz corruption trials, the *Examiner, Globe,* and *Chronicle* railed against Heney, and nightly, Heney's investigative reports were copied or stolen and furnished to attorneys for the United Railroads.

This view of Alcatraz Island may be similar to the last view enjoyed by Chief of Police William J. Biggy just before he mysteriously disappeared off the deck of a patrol boat on the night of November 30, 1908. Before Biggy's death, newspapers claimed that he was part of the Ruef gang and was complicit in the murder of Morris Haas in jail. Biggy denied the charges but considered resigning. On November 30, he crossed the bay at sundown to talk to Police Commissioner Hugo Keil at his home in Belvedere. Keil later said that he convinced Biggy to keep his job and that the chief had been in a cheerful mood near midnight when he cast off on the patrol boat for the return trip.

Only one other person, the pilot, Officer William Murphy, was aboard the patrol boat with Biggy. When the boat arrived in San Francisco, Biggy was gone. Murphy claimed that he last saw his boss leaning over the rail gazing at the view as they passed Alcatraz Island, and despite intense interrogation, gave no further information. Biggy's body was finally found floating near Angel Island on December 15. On the Sunday before Christmas, he was laid to rest after a funeral at St. Mary's Cathedral on Van Ness Avenue, attended by hundreds, including the entire force of the San Francisco Police Department.

Abe Ruef, shown here on the day he went to prison, March 8, 1911, was quoted by the *New York Times:* "My conscience is clear." Of the 40 individuals indicted in the Oliver Grand Jury report, only Ruef would ever serve serious jail time for his crimes. Schmitz's conviction was soon overturned on appeal, and others turned state's evidence to avoid prison. Ruef was sentenced to the maximum 14 years at San Quentin for bribery. Although *Bulletin* editor Fremont Older was instrumental in Ruef's indictment, he soon regretted his actions because of the severity of Ruef's sentence and the fact that others did not share in the punishment. Some suspected that anti-Semitism played a role in the sentencing. Older corresponded with Ruef and finally worked for his release, but Ruef served five years before being paroled. Although Eugene Schmitz later revived his political career, running unsuccessfully for mayor twice and succeeding in election to the board of supervisors, Ruef died on February 29, 1936, broke and forgotten by the town he once brilliantly controlled.

On Monday, May 6, 1907, strikers and sympathizers surrounded the United Railroad car barns on Turk and Fillmore streets. Patrick Calhoun of United Railroads, still enmeshed in the growing bribery scandal, imported experienced strikebreakers from the East Coast, and barbed wire barricades were put up to protect the strikebreakers inside. On May 7, six streetcars, one seen here with armed guards, left the car barn. A mob began to throw rocks and bricks at the cars, and gunfire erupted between guards and striking workers, who were shooting from nearby vacant lots. Strikebreakers inside retaliated by opening fire on the crowd. That day two people died and at least 20 were wounded. At the end of May, the Metal Trades Union negotiated an agreement for an eight-hour workday, the first in the nation, to be phased in by 1910. Striking laundry workers achieved a 51-hour week, with a decrease to 48 hours by 1910. Calhoun became the hero of capitalists for simultaneously standing up to the strikers and being prosecuted for bribery. But as the Streetcar Strike dragged on through the summer, new skirmishes resulted in a strikebreaker's death. The Carmen admitted defeat in March 1908 and turned in their charter. The end tally of the summer of "class warfare" was six deaths, 250 injuries directly attributable to the strike, and 25 more deaths and 900 injuries caused by streetcar accidents.

The SFPD's management was swept clean after the scandals of the Ruef-Schmidt corruption trials, the indictment and firing of Chief Jeremiah Dinan in 1907, and the mysterious death of Chief William Biggy in 1908. New Mayor Edward Taylor appointed Jesse B. Cook chief of police. Cook started out as an acrobat who joined the police force in Texas and San Diego before reaching San Francisco in the late 1880s. He served on the early Chinatown Squad, and during his term as chief introduced the Solo Motorcycle Unit. He retired in 1911 to become a police commissioner when Chief David White took over. White would soon introduce modern recordkeeping in the department. In this photo, Captain James Kelly heads the mounted police unit in 1911. The San Francisco Police Department Mounted Police unit, founded in 1872, is the second oldest in the country.

San Francisco rises once again in this view from a "captive airship" (meaning a tethered dirigible). At left is Alcatraz Island with the reconstructed Ferry Building tower visible at the end of Market Street.

OLD HABITS DIE HARD

(1910–1920)

Although corrupt administrators at City Hall and the police department were booted out after Abraham Ruef's conviction for bribery in 1911, there were other criminal consortiums in the city. Prostitution had proceeded unhindered for generations, and super-pimp Jerome Bassity, "King of the Tenderloin," planned to build a new brothel with rooms for 100 working girls. In the spring of 1909, pastor of St. Francis Roman Catholic Church Father Terence Caraher, the *San Francisco Globe* newspaper, and new chief of police Jesse B. Cook joined forces to thwart Bassity. Cook risked his job, upsetting the long tradition of payoffs that kept the vice lords in business. As police commissioner in 1912, Cook and reformers like Father Caraher and Donaldina Cameron of the Presbyterian Mission lead the charge to eradicate prostitution by supporting the Red Light Abatement Act of 1914, narrowly passed by supervisors, but not confirmed as constitutional by the state supreme court until 1917.

In a last-ditch effort, over 300 perfumed prostitutes in furs and finery descended on reformer Reverend Paul Smith at the Central Methodist Church during Sunday services on January 25, 1917. These "Magdelenes" asked how they could support their children if evicted. Unmoved, police blockaded the Barbary Coast on Valentines Day, refusing access to all males without proof of residence or business and giving prostitutes a few hours to collect their belongings. The 83 dives and brothels shut down that day were not the only ones in the city and they were certainly not the last, but the days of the bawdy Barbary Coast had ended.

Meanwhile, the worst terrorist act in the city's history, the Preparedness Day Parade Bombing on July 22, 1916, killed ten and injured 40. Growing antagonism between union leadership and the Hall of Justice led to two hasty trials and the conviction of two well-known labor leaders, Thomas Mooney and Warren K. Billings. On November 15, 1919, police evicted all International Workers of the World ("Wobblies") from the city of San Francisco.

As the decade closed, Doughboys, lucky survivors of the First World War, returned to cheering crowds. Unfortunately, they brought a killer strain of influenza with them that would chalk up at least 3,500 more casualties in San Francisco, and require unprecedented and largely ineffective new laws before the epidemic dissipated in 1919.

The haunts and dives of the Old Barbary Coast were blackened or destroyed in 1906. But it didn't take long for a new strip of saloons, dance halls, and melodeons (concert halls) to develop along the 400–700 blocks of Pacific Street and vicinity. The Hippodrome, seen in this photo from around 1908, was probably located at this time at 560 Pacific Avenue and was owned by the Schivo Brothers. The Thalia, a famous dance hall seen in the background of this photo, was owned by George "Red" Kelley. It would soon move to the other side of the street, as the Hippodrome did, and was for many years the largest dance hall on the Pacific Coast. In its heyday, 80 to 100 girls worked alongside double shifts of bartenders. It was the namesake of a much seedier pre-earthquake ancestor, a cheap saloon and dance hall in the Tenderloin at Mason and Turk streets.

The south side of the 500 block of Pacific Street is shown here quiet in the daylight hours around 1914. At far-right is the Bella Union, the most popular melodeon, or concert hall, on the Barbary Coast for 60 years. There were no pretty waiter girls, and although the female performers had to sell drinks and entertain gentlemen in curtained boxes, they were not prostitutes. Many vaudevillians, including Lotta Crabtree, got their start there or in other houses like the Olympic, the Pacific, Bert's New Idea, or the Adelphi. The Bella Union in later years was called the Haymarket Theater, then the Imperial Concert Hall, and ended as Eden Musee, a penny arcade and waxworks. At center is the elaborate entrance of the new Hippodrome, and at left is the Red Mill, formerly known as the Moulin Rouge, another popular dance hall owned by George Buckler.

A famous lightweight prizefighter in his youth, Spider Kelly opened a dance hall and bar after the earthquake on the 500 block of Pacific Street, pictured here around 1911. Next door, separated only by a flimsy wood partition, was a bar named Purcell's. Purcell's was a drinking man's joint, a real dive, and if a man didn't drink often, he was thrown out. Predictably, there were many fights at Purcell's, and bullets were known to rip through the partition, endangering Kelly's bartenders. So Kelly lined his back bar and mirror with sheet-iron boilerplate, and because bullets were not rare in his own establishment, Kelly similarly reinforced the front of his own bar. Captain Meagher of the Chicago police force visited the Barbary Coast in 1912 and claimed that San Francisco was more depraved than his hometown, noting Spider Kelly's as "undoubtedly the worst dive in the world." But he never made it to Purcell's.

While the main industries of the Old Barbary Coast were gambling, prostitution, and thievery (while drinking), the whole point of the post-earthquake Barbary Coast was drinking while dancing. In its last sodden hurrah, the Coast drew tremendous crowds to try out new West Coast moves, including the turkey trot, bunny hug, chicken glide, and the Texas Tommy. This 1911 photograph shows the interior of Spider Kelly's, which featured a live band whose tuxedoed members played a grand piano, trombone, trumpet, drums, and xylophone. At far-left, lifting a tasty toe on the dance floor, is "Little Egypt." She is probably not the original Little Egypt who took the city by storm in 1897 at the Midway Plaisance on Market Street, but a later imitator. This Little Egypt performed a "muscle dance" that included many interesting gyrations.

Located at 592 Pacific Avenue, the Moulin Rouge, or the Red Mill, was an elegantly decorated dance hall and saloon owned by the Parente Brothers. A tango seems to be gathering steam in this view recorded around 1911, and the fashionable attire for women appears to be trimly tailored suits and enormous hats.

In 1911, world heavyweight boxer Jack Johnson, seen here in one of his beloved sports cars with his wife, Etta Terry Duryea, stops in front of the Cliff House and streetcar terminal. Johnson was one year past his heavyweight-title win, and a favorite target of SFPD's new motorcycle unit, designed to catch "scorchers" and other reckless motorists. Once when stopped for a $50 ticket, Johnson handed the officer a $100 bill, telling him to keep the change as he intended to make the return trip at the same speed. Johnson later served time in Leavenworth for a trumped-up charge under the notorious Mann Act. He is rumored to have beaten Etta, who committed suicide in 1912. Although he lost his heavyweight title four years after this photo, he kept fighting until 1938 and finally died in a car crash in 1946. Jack Johnson was honest, fearless, and just plain bad. When asked to advise a journalist on the secret of his success with women, he answered, "Eat jellied eels and think distant thoughts."

A civic Reconstruction Committee, headed up by "Boss" Abe Ruef, came to the conclusion that Chinatown's real estate was too valuable to allow the Chinese to remain there after the earthquake and fire. While the committee dithered, however, Chinatown's Chinese Six Companies, the Empress of China, and hope of tax revenues convinced officials to allow Chinatown to rise again at the same location. With all municipal birth records destroyed in the fire, many Chinese men were now able to import wives and children. This eventually created a large number of middle-class families in Chinatown, decreasing the need for slave girls, opium, and gambling. Nevertheless, in its last years of rampant vice, Chinatown was even more plagued with tong warfare. The Chinatown Squad officers in 1911 were (left to right) Lieutenant Dan Sylvester, Charles E. Munn, Lieutenant H. Sylvester, Arthur McPhee, J. J. Cummings, Ed Plume, and L. P. H. Meyer.

Repeated waves of reform had washed over San Francisco's city government since the turn of the century, but none so strong as the reform measures in the wake of the Ruef-Schmidtz–era scandals. In 1913, the board of supervisors passed a Red-Light District resolution, effective in December of 1914, that would deal a deathblow to the Barbary Coast after it was finally upheld in the state supreme court in 1917. Similar measures were afoot in Chinatown, as attested by this very public opium bonfire put on by federal agents and local police officers in 1914. There was hope for many local opium addicts, however. A new drug to cure their dependence began to appear in San Francisco. It was called "heroin" for its ability to inspire heroic deeds.

This is a 1913 view of the front entrance of San Quentin State Prison, the oldest prison in the state. From its very inception, San Quentin was overcrowded, its first structure built between 1852 and 1854 by inmates of the packed prison ship *Waban,* anchored in the bay. That first cellblock, designed by architect Reuben Clark for 150 prisoners, soon held 250. Even after three new cellblocks were completed in the 1870s, a prison built for 444 had 915 inmates. Originally privately run, the prison leased labor, which caused so many deaths that the state took over in 1861. Folsom Prison, built to relieve overcrowding at San Quentin, began taking prisoners in 1880. San Quentin's prison population peaked in 1930 at 6,380. By the 1960s, San Quentin was the second largest prison in the United States. The administration building with a crenellated roof, seen here, was probably built in the 1880s.

This August 1, 1910, view of San Quentin State Prison shows the South Cellblock under construction in the background. The largest house at far-left is the warden's residence, and a small village, not visible here, housed prison staff and their families. At far-right is a long, three-story building, the window sash and blind factory. The third floor also held the gallows where prisoners were executed. Parallel to that structure is a lower row of two-story buildings. The building in the center of that row contains the oldest section of the prison, called "the Stones." The upper floor had 48 cells, holding four prisoners each, and the lower floor held the Long Room, a 160-foot-long dormitory, and the turnkey office. In 1858 (or 1854), a 14-cell dungeon was added on the north side that was used for 80 years for solitary confinement. The Stones was occupied until 1959, and the dungeon still exists. The building on the left in that row is a hospital, library, and chapel, refurbished in 1885.

This view looks south over the impeccably landscaped central courtyard of San Quentin Prison in 1910. The back of the administration building at the entrance is just visible at far-left. An electrical tower can be seen at right in the center of the garden. San Quentin had a well-earned reputation for brutality in its early days, when punishment included floggings with a rawhide strap, and shower baths in which naked prisoners were tied to ladders and then sprayed in the face and genitals with a high-pressure stream of cold water until, according to some accounts, blood burst from eyes and ears. In 1880, the last official flogging made way for solitary confinement in the dungeon, where each of 14 cells was sealed off with iron doors with a small slit known as a Judas Hole. Men slept on straw matting and used chamber buckets for waste. Warden Clinton Duffy finally banned flogging, solitary confinement in the dungeon, and torture for interrogation in 1944.

This is one of the "Old Spanish Prison" cellblocks, built in the 1870s. These buildings had cells that were accessed from an exterior balcony, a feature rarely seen in prison architecture. The cells, designed to hold four men, had no windows. This scene from July 1910 shows a Sunday morning "Unlock," when the cell doors were opened to let the prisoners out. The electrical tower and central garden are visible in the foreground.

The prison held both male and female inmates until 1932, and many pickpockets from the Barbary Coast spent time there. The women were housed in an old stone structure south of the administration building. This is the courtyard of the women's cellblock, which by 1913 featured an elaborate fountain. The female inmates were watched over by prison matrons.

In 1913, Warden James A. Johnston tried to shift the focus of the prison from punishment to rehabilitation, instituting classes and training for prisoners. Previously, the prisoners worked in industrial shops like the jute mill, tin shop, or window sash and blind factory, making products to sell to raise money for the prison. This mathematics class in 1913 was held in the schoolroom set up in the chapel.

This San Quentin Prison cell, photographed around 1913, is probably located in the South Cellblock, which was built in 1910. It would have been considered a modern marvel compared to the earliest cells in the 1854 structure known as the Stones, where the upper floor had 48 cells, two rows of 24 back-to-back. Cells measured only 5 feet 11 inches by 9 feet 10 inches, and held four prisoners each. There were no windows.

The corridor of the South Cellblock is seen here soon after it was constructed in 1910. In 1891, the state declared San Quentin and Folsom prisons to be the state's designated execution sites. The first hanging at San Quentin was in 1893. A total of 215 people died by hanging there until 1937, when the state legislature approved lethal gas in place of the noose. From that time on, San Quentin became the sole execution site in California. During the next six decades, 196 prisoners were gassed, including four women. Lethal injection was introduced in 1996.

This photograph captures a meal set out in the dining room, or mess hall, of San Quentin Prison around 1913. Supper appears to include a large square of bread topped by two crackers or slices of cheese, accompanied by large sausages. According to the caption of a similar photo in the Marin County Library collection, "Here occurred a bloody riot in 1911."

Famous detective Allan Pinkerton might have been the first to systematically use both the mug shot and the rogues' gallery when he opened his soon-to-be-famous Pinkerton National Detective Agency in 1850. Alphonse Bertillon systematized both the mug shot and crime photography in the 1880s, and New York City Police Department's Inspector Thomas Byrnes helped popularize the term rogues' gallery in the late 1880s. The words "mug," slang for face, and "rogue," originally meaning vagrant or tramp, date to eighteenth-century England. This 1912 scene shows a mug ripe for shooting in San Francisco.

Louis Laplace looks like a good candidate for a rogues' gallery, but his hobo outfit is a disguise. Laplace was the first undercover detective in San Francisco, detailed by Chief David White in February 1914 to infiltrate the army of "undesirables," who camped out in a vacant lot on Howard Street, south of Market Street. Laplace fit right in and lived in the hobo camp, rising to the rank of second-in-command and learning all their confidences, including detailed plans for robbery and mayhem. Each morning, Laplace reported to Chief White by secret messenger, laying out the details of the nefarious agendas. Wishing to apprehend the ringleader without blowing his cover, Laplace managed to talk the group into taking a trip to Sacramento, where the hobo leader was arrested.

Women were employed by the San Francisco Police Department before the turn of the century as clerical workers or as police matrons, wardens for women prisoners. In 1910, the Los Angeles Police Department hired the first policewoman in the country, Alice Stebbins Wells. By 1912, the LAPD had three policewomen, and major cities followed suit. In 1914, the San Francisco Police Department hired three policewomen, all named some variant of Catherine. So they became known as the "Three Kates." Seen here in 1928, 14 years after they were first hired, are Kate O'Conner and Kathlyn Sullivan.

When citizens realized they must prepare for inevitable participation in the global war, the Bay Area went all out to celebrate national Preparedness Day on July 22, 1916. This was the biggest parade ever held in San Francisco, with 51,329 marchers representing 2,134 Bay Area organizations, and 52 bands in a procession that would take 3.5 hours to pass. Although many labor leaders did not favor entering the war, newspaper, telephone, telegraph, and streetcar unions marched in the parade. Thomas Mooney, head of the Molders Union, was tipped off about possible violence at the parade, so he pushed a resolution through his union and the Central Labor Committee warning that a provocateur might try to harm the labor movement by disrupting the parade. Seen above is the view on Market Street between Kearny and Grant. The Sorenson Diamond street clock at right reads 2:40 P.M., over 30 minutes after a bomb exploded.

At 2:06 P.M., just 30 minutes after the Preparedness Day Parade had begun, a bomb placed in a suitcase exploded near the southwest corner of Steuart and Market streets. Here detectives and police are on the scene. The bomb maker, who used dynamite with metal sash weights to act as shrapnel, placed the bomb in a suitcase and left it on the sidewalk. The powder marks and hole on the brick wall in the background mark the spot where the bomb detonated. Ten people were killed and 40 wounded.

THINK !
ARBOR
OTEL
WHY?
IGAR
RES & BYRNE RUBBER CO.
FERRY HOUSE
ROOMS
THE
HARBOR
HOTEL
5¢
HAVISIDE, WITHER
SHIP CHANDLERS,
AGENTS WHITLOCK COR

The image above shows the bomb site near the southwest corner of Steuart and Market streets at right as a crowd begins to gather. The parade continued for some time, as participants were unaware of the events unfolding near the Ferry Building at the foot of Market Street. The bombing would become the worst terrorist act in San Francisco history. In the hysteria and paranoia that followed, well-known labor leader Thomas Mooney and his assistant Warren Billings were arrested.

Thomas Mooney and Warren K. Billings were tried for the Preparedness Day Bombing. Given the hysteria and paranoia following the most deadly terrorist attack ever to hit the city, as well as San Francisco's long history of labor unrest and political corruption, it is not surprising that the well-known labor leaders were convicted in hasty, incompetently managed trials. In the view above, District Attorney Charles M. Fickert addresses the jury in the Billings trial. Later, some charged that Fickert coerced and coached witnesses to testify against Mooney and Billings. One of Fickert's witnesses claimed to have seen the crime with her astral body. Mooney received a death sentence and Billings, life imprisonment. Intervention by President Woodrow Wilson in 1918 commuted Mooney's sentence to life imprisonment. It would be many years before either man would make headlines again.

Although three policewomen, the "Three Kates," had been hired in 1914, most women in the San Francisco Police Department just before World War I were either clerical workers or women who acted as social workers, sent out in the field to deal with women's issues like spousal abuse or prostitution. In this view, Police Chief David A. White and Judge John Sullivan talk over a case with a "lady worker" in 1917.

Women had been working as guards, or police matrons, in the city jail and prison since the 1890s. This 1917 view shows police matron Mrs. Condon with some of her prisoners in the women's department of the San Francisco City Prison.

The Old Barbary Coast harbored "deviates" of every stripe, and there are vague references to bars that catered to homosexuals. Dr. Magnus Hirschfeld coined the terms "transvestite" and "transsexual" at his clinic in Berlin in 1907 and 1919, respectively. It is doubtful that police officers would have been familiar with either word when transvestite Geraldine Portica, shown here in 1917, was hauled into the station. Geraldine, a Mexican citizen, claimed that he had been named and raised as a girl by his mother, and had spent his entire life as a female. He had been employed as a chambermaid on Sixth Street when he was arrested, and he was later deported to Mexico. Author Nan Alamilla Boyd traces the emergence of a larger San Francisco gay community to the end of World War II, when many gays and lesbians in the military in San Francisco were decommissioned, either honorably or dishonorably, if discovered.

Shown here in 1922, Ernest Long, chief engineer on the steamship *Rose Mar,* was arrested for "impersonating a woman," a crime he executed with skill and panache. Both Geraldine Portica and Ernest Long had much more elegant mug shots than were normally accorded criminals. Police officers probably allowed press photographers access to cover such novelties for their readers. By 1949, scandal sheets like the short-lived *The Truth* blared on July 11, "Homos Invade S. F." The long road to a greater public acceptance and decriminalization of gay and transgender men and women would shadow the civil rights movement, still decades away.

San Francisco seemed to dodge the influenza bullet that hit the country in the spring of 1918. Some health officials predicted it would not even reach the West Coast. Therefore, the city was not prepared when the first case struck on September 24. Patriotic rallies and parades may have contributed to the flu's spread during September, and by mid-October, there were 4,000 known cases in the city. So unprepared were medical personnel that doctors and the Red Cross could respond to only half of the calls for help that they received. Brave volunteers did their best to stand in for trained personnel and comfort the grieving. A largely useless law was passed requiring citizens to wear gauze masks in public, and schools, theaters, and other public venues closed. This photograph is captioned, "Say! Young Fellow, Get a mask or go to jail."

City officials came up with a rhyme to encourage citizens to wear their masks: "Obey the laws, and wear the gauze. Protect your jaws from septic paws." Although the influenza epidemic had a tendency to strike healthy, young people, getting young folks to wear masks was not always easy. In this staged publicity still, a policeman loses his patience with a young man who has lowered his mask to have a smoke, saying, "Ah! Come on and tell it to the Judge." A siren's wail on November 21, 1918, signaled that citizens could remove their masks, and theaters and schools reopened. The call was premature, as two more waves of flu, less severe than the first, finally resulted in over 3,500 fatalities.

Local labor strikes became a way of life in San Francisco and across the nation. A telephone operators' strike in 1907 in San Francisco had preceded the bloody Streetcar Strike. Now, in 1919, San Francisco's telephone operators joined a national strike. They are seen here congregating on Bush Street in front of the main telephone company office. The marquee of the Old Poodle Dog Restaurant can be seen two doors down the street. Although strikes in this era were often violent, these ladies, in their fashionable hats and white gloves, waving to passing motorists, do not look likely to toss any weighted handbags at anyone's head.

In this photograph, a police officer protectively escorts a strikebreaker into Pacific Telephone and Telegraph's main headquarters on Bush Street during the telephone operators' strike of 1919. The *New York Times* reported on July 22, 1919, that the union officials in Washington, D.C., asked San Francisco operators to return to work, and other Pacific Coast unions did likewise.

Although it does not look secure by modern standards, this was the new "shotgun station" on Junipero Serra Boulevard in 1919. Police Chief David A. White, at right, looks on as an officer inspects one of the shotguns that were a new addition to the SFPD arsenal. The police telephone call box can be seen at right.

By October 20, 1920, the date of this photograph, San Francisco's population had grown to over half a million. It was clear that the San Francisco Police Department, shown here during its annual review, had also grown. The department would face challenges in the years ahead during the decade of prohibition, gangsters, and tong wars. In the front row from left to right are Secretary Charles F. Skelly, police commissioners Jesse B. Cook and Dr. T. E. Shumate, President Theodore J. Roche, Mayor James Rolph, Jr., Chief of Police David A. White, and Chief Clerk Daniel O'Brien. O'Brien would soon take over as chief of police.

Falling Stars and Penny-ante Gangsters

(1920–1929)

San Franciscans hardly missed a beat when Prohibition changed the tune. Although drinking moved underground, Irish Catholics ran the Hall of Justice, and their Prohibition enforcement lacked zeal. Arrests made for show were not prosecuted. The SFPD also declined all invitations to entertain Sicilians engaged in "Black Hand" extortion. Crime lords from the East were greeted on their arrival and booked on trains out of town the next day. The era that spawned gangland warfare in other cities created frustrated G-men, fabulous speakeasies, tong wars, and penny-ante gangsters in San Francisco.

The Tenderloin in the twenties, rife with gambling halls, billiard parlors, boxing gyms, theaters, restaurants with cellar speakeasies, and sizzling nightlife, was a Noir playground. It inspired the fiction of author Dashiell Hammett, who lived at 891 Post Street, the address assigned to Sam Spade in *The Maltese Falcon.*

Chinatown was the one neighborhood not controlled by the SFPD, and it erupted in bloody street warfare as tongs fought for control of gambling, opium, and slave girls. Detective Sergeant Jack Manion, the model for Hammett's character Sam Spade, had the difficult task of leading the Chinatown Squad in 1921 and is credited with finally taming the tongs and ending female slave trafficking by 1926.

San Franciscans did not need the movies or mafia for excitement. A string of high profile murder trials unfolded in late 1920 with some small-time hoodlums called the Howard Street Gang. A gang rape of several girls initiated a series of events leading to the murder of two well-regarded SFPD detectives and the Sonoma County sheriff. That would spark a reprisal, the second-to-last lynching in the West. The next summer brought the kidnapping and murder of a Catholic priest and the dramatic conviction of his killer with the help of a new invention, the polygraph, or lie detector. And just one month later, news surfaced about Hollywood actress Virginia Rappe, dead after a scandalous drunken bash at the St. Francis Hotel over Labor Day weekend. Indicted for her rape and murder was none other than Roscoe "Fatty" Arbuckle, one of Hollywood's first superstars.

In 1926, Clarence "Buck" Kelly went on a murderous heroin-fueled rampage through the streets of San Francisco, and Joe Tanko, who had been on a three-year crime spree, was finally taken down in a seedy San Francisco apartment where he was spending his days playing penny-ante poker.

Although Prohibition, enacted in 1919 to prohibit the manufacture, transport, and sale of alcohol, caused a spike in gangland crime throughout the country, it did not have a drastic effect on San Francisco. With Irish Americans filling the majority of positions of power in the civil service and police department, the Sicilian mafia, or "Black Hand" as it was known locally, never got a strong foothold in the Bay Area. But the SFPD had their own local gangs to deal with, so they took advantage of the training offered by these marines, fresh from a world war, in the use of the machine gun on September 18, 1920.

The San Francisco Police Department's first taste of the Roaring Twenties came on November 27, 1920, in the South of Market area around Howard Street, where for years hobos and bums had camped on vacant lots or in shacks. A gang that included small-time boxers Spud Murphy and Edward "K .O." Kruvosky had moved into a little house at 1256 1/2 Howard Street, shown above. According to Charles Foster, a retired police officer who joined the force in 1920, the Howard Street Gang ran a bootlegging operation out of a South of Market warehouse. On November 27, the gang lured several young girls into their clubhouse and gang raped or assaulted them. One of the women, Jean Stanley, managed to escape when the men fell asleep, and she brought back the police.

THEFT

With San Quentin in its front yard and Alcatraz Military Prison in its backyard, San Francisco was ready in 1920 for a restaurant called the Dungeon, at 47 Anna Lane, just above Ellis and Powell streets. A mural on the back wall shows a prison yard, while cells complete with bunks feature various crimes, including the new crime of bootlegging. The name may have come from the famous dungeon at San Quentin, built in the 1850s and used until 1944 for solitary confinement of prisoners.

The police caught some of the Howard Street Gang, but three others, George Barron (also known as Boyd), Terry Fitts, and Charles Valento escaped. K. O. Kruvosky struck a fighting pose, but was K.O.'d himself by Officer Ed Darling. Kruvosky is also remembered for being largely responsible for a subsequent four-month ban on professional boxing in San Francisco. Shown here are three of the girls who were assaulted by the gang, photographed at a later date outside the Santa Rosa Courthouse. From left to right, they are Jessie Montgomery, Pearl Hanley, and Edna Fulmer.

It is rumored that several Sonoma County detectives were drinking at the Toscano Hotel (later Guidotti's, Michelle's, and Stark's Steak House) in the old Italian District in Santa Rosa, when they were tipped off that the escaped Howard Street Gang members were hiding in a house in the back of the hotel at 28 West Seventh Street, shown above. On December 6, San Francisco detectives Lester Dorman and Miles Jackson and policewoman Katherine O'Conner (taken along to handle a woman traveling with the suspects) joined Sonoma County Sheriff ("Sunny Jim") James Petray, and together they approached the house. The three police officers entered and placed two suspects under arrest. A third suspect on the couch rose with a revolver and shot Officer Dorman and Sheriff Petray dead. Sergeant Jackson, who was in another room, rushed toward the sound of gunfire and was also shot. Before he died, Sergeant Jackson was able to wound a fourth suspect.

All four suspects were arrested later that day and brought to the jail in the Sonoma County Courthouse on Fourth Street, shown above in December 1920. An agitated group of men gather outside. The two San Francisco detectives who died, Lester Dorman and Miles Jackson, had been on the force for six years. Slain Sonoma County Sheriff "Sunny" Jim Petray was a popular man from Healdsburg, a fruit buyer before being elected sheriff in 1918. On the evening of December 9, the day of the San Francisco officers' funeral, a caravan of 12 to 15 cars left the small town of Healdsburg in northwestern Sonoma County, headed for the county courthouse in Santa Rosa. According to reliable eyewitness accounts, the group took pseudo-military titles and was led by "Captain" Fred Young, a local mortician and funeral home director in Healdsburg.

On the evening of December 9, 1920, all three of the male suspects, George Barron (Boyd), Terry Fitts, and Charles Valento, were dragged from the Sonoma County jail and taken to the Franklin Cemetery in Santa Rosa, where they were hung from a scraggly oak tree. This photo, credited to *San Francisco Chronicle* reporter Bornsmuller, records the second-to-last lynching in the West. Car headlamps illuminated the scene. Rumors of complicity by SFPD members have never been substantiated. It has been established that the instigators were good friends of Sheriff Petray from the town of Healdsburg. The identity of the lynch mob leader, Fred Young, later Sonoma County Coroner from 1926 to 1940, was a closely guarded secret among a select few for eight decades.

Although they did not realize it at the time, the luckiest of the Howard Street Gang were boxers Spud Murphy and K. O. Kruvosky, who were arrested at their shack on Howard Street on November 27, 1920. They were tried for the rape of the young women, convicted, and sentenced to San Quentin. In this photograph, the leader of the Howard Street Gang, Spud Murphy, poses with his mother during a trial that garnered additional publicity because of the dramatic events that unfolded in Santa Rosa soon after the raid on their hideout. Spud was released from San Quentin in the late 1930s, only to become involved in a marijuana drug bust in 1939.

On the night of August 2, 1921, a stranger
wearing a motorist's muffler and goggles knocked
at Father Patrick E. Heslin's rectory in Colma, just
south of San Francisco. The man asked the priest
to accompany him in a motorcar to administer
last rites to a dying man. The priest quickly
complied, carrying with him the Eucharist. The
next day a letter arrived at St. Mary's Cathedral
in San Francisco demanding $6,500 in ransom
for the return of Father Heslin. A week later
a man named William A. Hightower, shown
here, presented himself at Archbishop Hanna's
residence in San Francisco, claiming that he had
information that entitled him to the $8,000
reward being offered for the recovery of Father
Heslin, dead or alive. Bishop Hanna was skeptical
and told Hightower to come back the next day.

An *Examiner* reporter, George Lynn, happened to be at Bishop Hanna's house when William Hightower arrived. Smelling a story, Lynn brought the reward claimant, dressed in a "rumpled Palm Beach suit and a wide, floppy straw hat," to the *Examiner* office. Hightower subsequently led Lynn, a photographer, Chief of Police Daniel O'Brien, and Constable S. A. Landini of Colma to a spot at Salada Beach (now Sharp Park in Pacifica) where Father Heslin's corpse, buried at the foot of a billboard on the beach, was recovered. The photograph above records that scene on August 10, 1921. Hightower returned to the office where the editor placed guards, ordering that no one leave the building until daybreak. Because the newspaper had broken the case, the police complied.

The next day the *Examiner* published four full pages on Father Heslin's murder. Here San Francisco detectives inspect evidence near Salada Beach on August 10, 1921. William Hightower was one of the first criminals to be tested with a new instrument invented by Canadian psychologist John Larson, who was working for the Berkeley Police Department. The device recorded the combined measurement of respiration and blood pressure on a drum of smoked paper. He called it a polygraph, and it would soon become the much-touted lie detector, used even to the present day. Hightower failed the test, and newspapers around the country, including the *New York Times,* heralded a new era in crime investigation.

Detectives hardly needed the polygraph to solve the Heslin case. The priest's housekeeper identified Hightower as the man who came to the door on August 2, and sand matching the burial site was found on Hightower's shoes and knife. Professor C. Eisenshunel, handwriting expert and coroner of the city and county of San Francisco, shown here in 1921, testified that Hightower wrote the ransom letter. John Larson used his polygraph again in 1922 to clear Henry Wilkens, accused of having arranged the murder of his own wife in a fake car robbery while their children watched from the back seat. Wilkens was thought by many to be guilty, and so San Francisco police vowed never to use the polygraph again. Larson soon came to distrust his own invention for lie detection and spent his entire career attempting to use the device to diagnose mental illness.

Hightower was convicted on October 13, 1921, and sentenced to life imprisonment at San Quentin. Father Patrick Heslin had been much loved at Sacred Heart Parish in Turlock before being transferred to Holy Angels Parish in Colma. His large funeral at St. Mary's Cathedral in San Francisco is shown here. William A. Hightower became a chef at San Quentin, and he was paroled on May 20, 1965, at the age of 86, after 26 requests for parole had been denied. Hightower is sometimes called the "flapjack murderer" because of his chosen burial site beneath an Albers Rolled Oats billboard showing a man cooking pancakes.

Although the Barbary Coast had been forced out of business in 1917, Chinatown continued to do a brisk trade in opium, extortion, murder, and brothels. The tongs that controlled the trade had grown and multiplied. They also continued to traffick in human flesh, consigning young girls to lives of misery for profit. Police Chief Daniel O'Brien was appointed in 1920, and he in turn appointed a boyhood pal, Jack Manion, to head the Chinatown Squad. For the next 26 years, Manion's hardboiled, straight-shooting personality allied itself to Chinatown, and incidentally became the inspiration for much of the pulp fiction of the twenties and thirties. Manion succeeded in doing what all before him could not: negotiate a peace among the warring tongs that had made violent reprisal a way of life. He could not have done it without winning the trust of Chinatown. Here the warring Hip Sing and Ping Koong tongs negotiate a peace in February 1921.

The Peace Meeting of 1921 between the warring tongs was just a beginning of the crime cleanup in Chinatown. Manion successfully overcame cultural and language barriers to build a network of Chinese informants who worked with him to limit gambling and drugs networks, and finally, after 70 long years, he provided the axe and the brawn that Presbyterian missionary Donaldina Cameron needed to shut down slave girl traffic. By 1930, Jack Manion was ripe for promotion, but had become such an institution that the Chinese community requested that he stay, which he did until he retired in 1946. This photograph documents the final days of the headquarters of the Hop Sing tong in September 1929.

Roscoe Conkling Arbuckle overcame a tragic childhood to become one of the most popular and highly paid comedians of silent films. Roscoe's father abused him and openly doubted that Roscoe was his son. By the age of 12, the year his mother died and his father abandoned him, Roscoe weighed 185 pounds. Yet he had a clear soprano voice and was remarkably agile. While working odd jobs at a San Jose hotel, Roscoe won a talent contest, then managed to pick up vaudeville gigs around the country. He landed his first film role back in California in 1909, the same year he married singer Minta Durfee. His rise to fame from that point on was phenomenal, and during the next decade, he would mentor both Charlie Chaplin and Buster Keaton and start his own film company, producing some of the best silent films in Hollywood. "Fatty" Arbuckle appears above with Jane Acker in a publicity still from the 1920 film *The Roundup.*

By 1920, Arbuckle had turned over his film company to Buster Keaton so that he could accept Paramount's offer of one million a year, an astronomical sum at that time. Despite his commercial success, Roscoe suffered from health problems and had developed a drinking problem, though his affection for alcohol was not uncommon in Hollywood during that era. He and wife Minta had separated in 1917. On September 3, 1921, Arbuckle, exhausted by his film schedule, motored with friends, director Fred Fischbach and actor Lowell Sherman, for a Labor Day holiday weekend at the elegant St. Francis Hotel in San Francisco, seen above illuminated in 1919. They checked into three rooms, one of which was reserved for entertaining. On Monday, September 5, 1921, a party took place that included 25-year-old starlet Virginia Rappe and Bambina Maude Delmont. Fischbach's bootlegger provided the alcohol.

During the carousing and drinking on September 5, 1921, bit player Virginia Rappe, pictured at right around 1920, ended up vomiting and in pain in the bathroom of Fatty Arbuckle's room. Rappe was later seen by the hotel's doctor, who determined that she was simply inebriated, and later still, her companion Maude Delmont summoned another doctor who administered morphine. Finally, on September 8, another physician summoned by Delmont examined Rappe, and she was admitted to Wakefield Sanitarium that day. She died the next afternoon, and an illegal autopsy was performed from which it was determined that she had died of peritonitis from a burst bladder. Her organs were preserved in jars, making an autopsy by police impossible. Maude Delmont immediately filed a complaint against Arbuckle, claiming he had raped Virginia Rappe and mortally injured her.

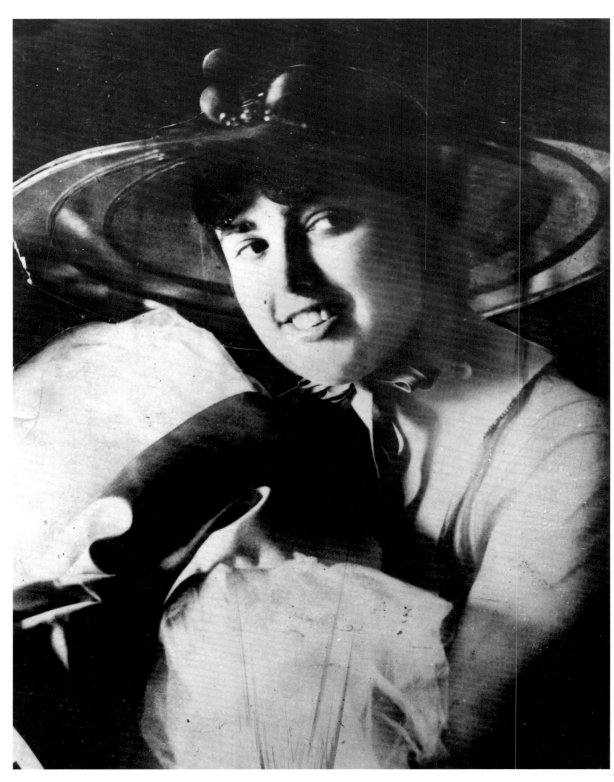

According to author James Robert Parish, Virginia Rappe had several abortions by age 16 and one child she gave away at birth, and he suggests that she was in San Francisco to obtain yet another abortion. She was known in Hollywood to drink heavily and act unpredictably, tearing off her clothes and screaming when drunk. Bambina Maude Delmont, it was later discovered, had a long history of racketeering, bigamy, fraud, and extortion. Even though Delmont's many conflicting statements to reporters and to San Francisco District Attorney Matthew Brady had been proven false by the time of the coroner's inquest on September 12, the ambitious prosecutor, who hoped one day to be governor, forged ahead. After all, he had already been quoted in the newspapers, saying he would prosecute to the fullest extent of the law. Roscoe "Fatty" Arbuckle is seen above being booked into city prison in San Francisco in September 1921. He was later released on bail.

Arbuckle shakes hands with Lieutenant Boland before he is released on bail. The William Randolph Hearst–owned newspaper chain set off like dogs after a bone, broadcasting lurid headlines and stories and portraying the shy, alcoholic entertainer as an uncouth lecher. The *Los Angeles Times*'s supportive accounts were no match for the Hearst publicity machine, and Arbuckle had been ruined in the press before the first of three trials even began. Some claim that Hearst vilified Arbuckle and portrayed the Hollywood film community as a cesspool of debauchery because he wanted to establish the movie-making industry in San Francisco instead of Los Angeles. Hearst was quoted as saying that the case made his papers more money than the sinking of the *Lusitania*.

Given the lack of medical evidence and conflicting accusations by Delmont (Brady wisely refused to let her testify), the judge might not have let the Arbuckle case go to trial at all without party guest Zey Prevon testifying that Rappe said "Roscoe hurt me" on her deathbed. The judge decided that Arbuckle (front-left) could be charged with first-degree murder, later reduced to manslaughter. Three separate trials were to follow, and women reportedly crowded the halls and courtroom of each one, even though they are not apparent in this 1921 photograph. By the time the third trial began in March of 1922, most of District Attorney Matthew Brady's evidence and testimony had been discredited. At the second trial, Prevon claimed that she had been coerced to lie by Brady, and when the third trial began, she had already fled the country. It took six minutes for the jury to finally acquit Arbuckle, and they spent five of those minutes drafting an apology.

When Roscoe "Fatty" Arbuckle was acquitted in April 1922, he had spent his fortune on his defense and had lost his house and cars. A few days later, the Hays Commission banned his films, and although the ban was eventually lifted, his film career never recovered. Some now believe it likely that Virginia Rappe died of medical incompetence and neglect following complications from an abortion. Maude Delmont, who set the circus in motion, toured the country giving performances as "The woman who signed the murder charge against Arbuckle," lecturing on the evils of Hollywood. Arbuckle, whose first wife Minta remained his lifelong friend and called him the nicest man in the world, married twice more. But his alcoholism only deepened. He died of a heart attack on June 29, 1933, just as his career seemed on the verge of a comeback. He is shown here, waving to the camera that loved him, on April 15, 1927.

Along with the polygraph, invented by Berkeley Police Department employee John Larson in 1921, handwriting analysis, and good old-fashioned investigation, detectives now had fingerprinting to add to their toolkit. Used in the United States for criminal identification since 1906, fingerprinting had become increasingly important to police and supplanted the cumbersome and sometimes unreliable Bertillon System. In this view, police photographers George Blum (left) and Detective Sergeant A. Jewel examine a fingerprint camera in March 1922.

Police Chief Daniel O'Brien instituted the first police academy in the nation in 1923. This academy trained both veteran and new officers. In this view, some of San Francisco's finest and fittest stand at attention for inspection at the academy in May 1923. Standing left to right in black suits are Chief of Police Daniel J. O'Brien, Police Commissioner Jesse B. Cook, and future chief, Captain William J. Quinn.

On September 8, 1925, Police Chief Daniel O'Brien described his 14-week training academy in the *News-Call Bulletin*: "The course consists of instructions in the proper method of breathing, walking, talking, running, jumping, swimming, life-saving, resuscitation, boxing, wrestling, military drilling, instructions in the handling of revolvers, rifles, shotguns, and singing. The instruction in singing is an innovation in police work, and was prescribed for the purpose of inculcating poise in the recruit. The recruit is compelled on his first appearance in the school, and on each succeeding appearance to go before the class and sing a song." Seen here in 1924 at an academy boxing session are, from left to right, Corporal H. Reilly, George Page, Vernon Van Matre, and E. Dathe.

Keeping up with gangsters who made use of automobiles, shotguns, and even machine guns was the job of San Francisco Police Department's shotgun detail, seen here in September 1925. They are, from left to right, George O'Leary, C. Keck, Fred Smith, and P. Backaracco. The Willard Hotel can be seen in the background, indicating that these officers have just gassed up at the corner of Willard and McAllister streets.

This handsome boxer is captioned "Our Police Dog, November 4, 1924 Election Day." The cape the dog wears bears the slogan "Vote Yes 41," referring to Proposition 41, a proposal to raise the salaries of select officers and members of the police department. It passed with 51 percent of the vote. This dog, probably more of a mascot than a police dog, apparently did his job well. According to the proposition, police salaries in 1924 were as follows:

Subordinate officers of the Police Department shall consist of Captains, who shall receive an annual salary of $3600; Lieutenants, $3000; Sergeants, $2640; Corporals, $2580; Captain of Police, $5000; Detective Sergeants, $2760; Captain of Police (over officers detailed for traffic duty), $4000; Police Officers, $2400 each; Police Patrol Drivers, $2400 each; Police Surgeon, $2400; Chief of Police, $7200; Chief Clerk and Property Clerk, $3600 each; Photographer, $2700.

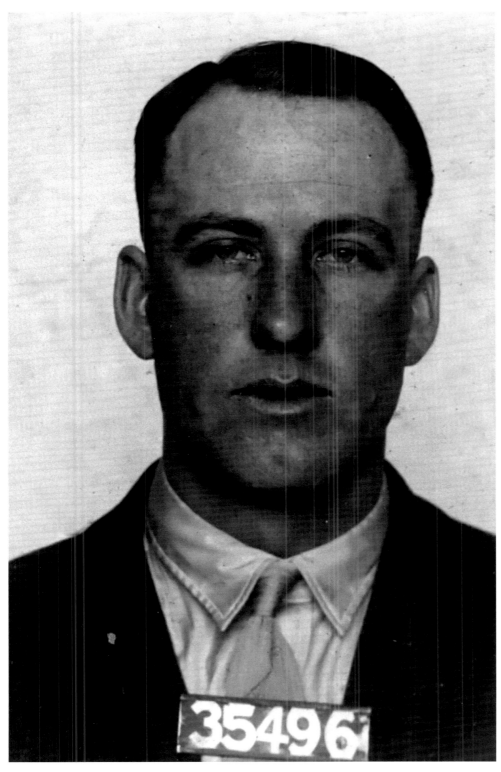

Ernest Granville Booth (a.k.a. Roy Reeves) was born in Oakland in 1898, the son of a prominent journalist. He began his own life's work at age 13, advancing from house burglary to finally earning a life sentence at Folsom by robbing an Oakland bank. At Folsom, he became a popular author when editor H. L. Mencken put his stories in the *American Mercury*. But to many, Booth's derangement was evident, and even his editors felt more comfortable while he was resident at the Big House. At Folsom, Booth spent so much time feigning illness in the infirmary that he contracted tuberculosis. His story "Ladies of the Mob" would bring Dashiell Hammett his first screenwriting credit. Booth was paroled in 1937, having spent 23 of his 39 years in prison, then lived in Placerville, California. During the next decade, he was questioned about a number of crimes, including the murder of wealthy socialite Florence Stricker, but was released for lack of evidence. It was not until 1947 that he was arrested in Hollywood for armed robbery and later charged with a series of robberies stretching from Seattle to Pasadena. Sentenced to 20 years in San Quentin, he finally died there of tuberculosis, probably in the late 1950s.

Police detectives needed a truck to fit all the loot recovered from an apartment at 3808 17th Street on June 12, 1924. The haul was valued at $6,000. Standing from left to right are Detective James Mitchell, Officer J. Barrickio, Detective Sergeant Leo Brenner, and Officer John Evatt. Seated in the truck is Sergeant George McLaughlin, and an unidentified man sits in the back.

When a statewide initiative to prohibit the manufacture, transport, and sale of alcohol was narrowly defeated in California in 1914, *Sunset Magazine* declared it a victory for the California wine industry and "San Francisco's robust thirst." Locally, 83 percent of San Franciscans voted against the initiative. Women first voted nationally in the November presidential election of 1920, and by that time, the Eighteenth Amendment to the Constitution had already become law. A state Prohibition Enforcement Act had been very narrowly defeated in 1920. This parade, held on November 4, 1922, supported a second state Prohibition Enforcement Act, which finally passed by a 52 percent to 48 percent vote. This view looks east on Market from O'Farrell Street toward the intersection of Kearny and Third streets.

Much of San Francisco's homemade hooch came from the basement stills of the Italian community or from hundreds of stills scattered in the rural Bay Area counties, Sonoma, Marin, Solano, and San Mateo. Surrounding counties supplied mostly low-grade grain alcohol, transported in cars or trucks that had secret compartments in the floor or seats. If necessary, it would be transferred to small boats to cross the bay. These armed bootleggers were more in danger of being highjacked by other bootleggers than being caught by police or federal agents. High-quality gin or bourbon came by ship from Canada to the San Mateo coast, especially Half Moon Bay. And of course "sacramental wines" produced by the wineries of Napa and Sonoma counties somehow found their way into some very unholy joints. This primitive still was hidden among tall reeds and grass in San Francisco.

Federal Agents stand amid cases of Scotch whiskey in the hold of a "rumrunner" captured by the USS *Seneca* in 1924. These runners helped supply at least 1,492 establishments selling alcohol in San Francisco, according to author James Smith. Federal agents could capture the bootleggers, but District Attorney Matthew Brady would not prosecute them. Historian Charles Fracchia states that there were speakeasies in almost every building in North Beach. According to journalist Warren Hinckle, if speakeasy operator Shanty Malone got raided, he just picked up and moved his operation to an empty apartment that he kept solely for that purpose. Word of mouth would bring his customers to the new location. According to these men, San Franciscans enjoyed the best quality booze in the country. During the "Dry Years," San Francisco was all wet.

The Sir Francis Drake Hotel opened in 1928 during an era of grandeur that would soon come to an end. Along with amenities such as an indoor golf course and radios in every room, guests had useful boxes installed in their doors that allowed objects—like bottles—to be delivered and received discreetly. A speakeasy between the first and second floors could be reached only with a special key on one hotel elevator. Other hotels around town also kept their illegal amenities hidden from authorities. A mezzanine bar at the Chancellor Hotel was never raided due to a constant lookout. The St. Francis Hotel put its nightclub in the basement. At the Palace Hotel, a visitor could send out for flowers, and the box would be delivered to his room with a bottle inside. The Plush Room speakeasy at the York Hotel could only be reached by going through a door across the street that led to a tunnel. The Warfield Theater even had a basement speakeasy.

The Customs Service confiscated this fleet of rumcraft in San Francisco on May 14, 1925, but there were plenty more. According to many accounts, local police watched over the bootlegging operations and speakeasies themselves. Although they may have accepted bribes, they did a good job of keeping out the Sicilian mafia that plagued other cities. If a crime boss showed up, he was greeted at the station and booked on a train out of town the next morning. According to author Dick Boyd, at least one Sicilian "naughty boy," Joe Parente, got a piece of the action in North Beach selling booze, but was soon "bumped off."

This neatly landscaped structure was the north end of the San Francisco County Jail in Balboa Park, at Ocean and San Jose streets. Flowerbeds in the foreground appear to indicate the year, 1925, and workmen on the roof may be prisoners who are painting the domed tower. This building was razed and the bricks were used to build sewers and gutters, part of a street-widening WPA Work Project (no. 1929) sometime between 1935 and 1939.

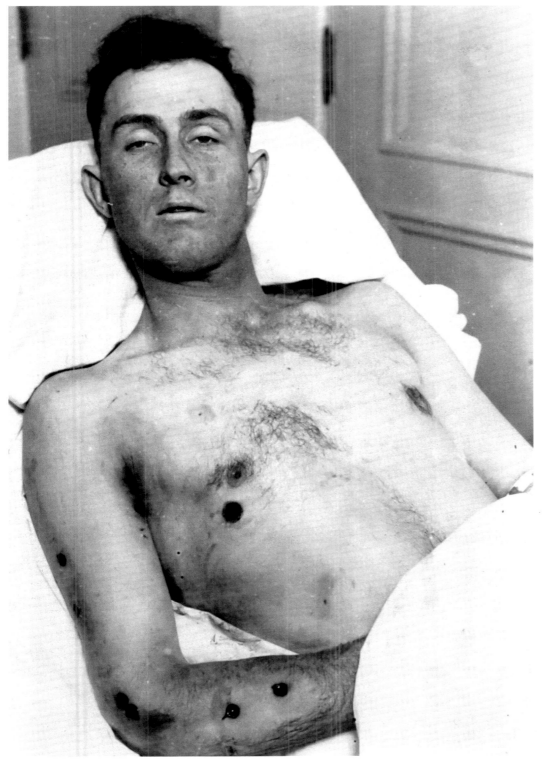

Fred Clarence Edgeller was known as the "Whistling Bandit" because he whistled a tune as he walked up to gas stations to rob them. He held up several gas stations in San Francisco before he was shot by SFPD Officer T. Herring on January 27, 1926, at Second and Howard streets. Before he died, the Whistling Bandit identified himself as Clarence Watson. When the coroner's office fingerprinted him, it was discovered that he was actually Fred Edgeller, who as a boy had served time at the Industrial School, a reform school for runaways in Kearney, Nebraska. Since leaving the school, he had been arrested several times for burglaries in Omaha and California, just another of the thousands of repeat criminals who used to roam the country using aliases, but were now tracked by fingerprinting.

In 1926, San Franciscans were shocked by a new type of crime, almost certainly fueled by heroin, the drug that had been marketed until 1910 as a cure for opium and morphine addiction and remained legal until 1924. On October 9, 1926, Clarence (Buck) Kelly was with Lawrence Weeks when he killed Mario Pagano in North Beach. Two days later, 23-year-old Kelly and 17-year-old Michael Papadaches hailed a taxi driven by Walter Swanson, then shot him on16th Street. They drove his taxi to Third Street, held up a gas station, then drove to San Bruno Road, where Kelly killed Mike Petrovich after asking him for the time. At Brannan and Seventh streets, they held up yet another gas station and killed John Duane, a night watchman. Moving across the street to a restaurant, Kelly shot the proprietor. Continuing up Brannan Street to Third Street, the pair held up a pedestrian, then proceeded to the waterfront where they managed two more hold ups. In all, Kelly was charged with four counts of murder, two charges of assault to commit murder, two charges of robbery, one charge of assault to rob, and a charge of grand larceny. Clarence Kelly's father, Joseph, sat silently in his own cell at San Quentin while his son was hanged. The elder Kelly was serving time for a robbery in Alameda County.

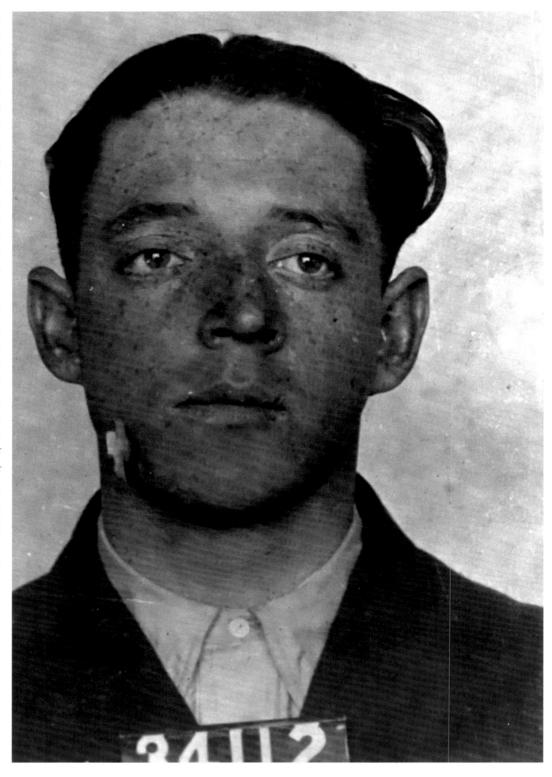

When he heard about the Buck Kelly killing spree in October of 1926, a small-time thug named Joe Tanko, hiding out in San Francisco, told his companions that he hated that kind of senseless killing. Joe's own crime story began on September 18, 1923, when San Bruno Police Chief Arthur Meehan saw a suspect vehicle and gave chase on his motorcycle. The car, driven by Tanko, ran Meehan off the road in front of San Bruno City Hall, and as the officer lay hurt on the ground, the car's passenger, Floyd Hall, got out and shot the officer repeatedly. Despite an armed vigilante force that searched the area, the suspects escaped, and Meehan died two days later. But Joe made the mistake of bragging about his recent robberies and the murder to his half-brother Frank, who tipped off the police. Both Tanko and Hall were picked up in Los Angeles, and because they confessed to the crimes, they avoided the death penalty and were sentenced to life in San Quentin. They nearly escaped on their way to prison by overcoming the guards, and they made a successful escape a year later by picking a lock and sliding down the wall on a jute rope.

Over the next several days, posses of armed police officers and citizens scoured the North Bay, where Tanko and Hall continued a crime spree by burglarizing stores in Petaluma and Healdsburg and carjacking a man in Santa Rosa. Then they turned up in Sacramento, where over the course of days, they chalked up another four holdups, three carjackings, and one murder, as well as wounding police officer Clyde Nunn. To call less attention to themselves, the convicts split up, but Hall was betrayed by a friend on May 15 for the $1,000 reward money. Tanko, after holing up in an opium den in Sacramento, made his way to Colorado, where he lived for a while by robbery. Why Joe Tanko chose to return to San Francisco where police knew him is anyone's guess. By the fall of 1926, he was holed up at the apartment of a friend, Theodore ("Creepy") Wilson, at 1378 McAllister Street (above), playing penny-ante poker.

When four officers arrived at 1378 McAllister Street on November 13, 1926, they had no idea that Joe Tanko was inside with the others. The officers surrounded the apartment, and Detective Sergeant Van Matre called through the window to tell the occupants to put their hands up. The others might have complied, but Joe Tanko, lying on the bed out of sight, shot Van Matre in the groin, then broke for the stairway to the upper floor, where Sergeant Roney ordered Tanko to halt. Without hesitation, Tanko shot him in the stomach. But Roney managed to return fire, hitting Tanko five times and firing so close that he set Tanko's clothes on fire. Soon crowds had assembled in the street to gape at the "Death Flats," and over the next several days, 10,000 citizens lined up to pass through the coroner's office for the chance to see Joe Tanko's body. Many said he was smaller than they expected.

When it comes to crime, nothing is sacred. Here the San Francisco Police Department displays vestments and chalices stolen from Catholic churches in California during the year 1928. The holy loot, valued at over $50,000, was found in an antique store at 1312 Haight Street by Detective Sergeant M. Mitchell. When thief R. J. Ganer was apprehended, he claimed that he had just picked it all up in Mexico.

During Prohibition, rumrunners had a fairly easy time evading local police for one simple reason: they had faster boats. By August 1929, however, the San Francisco Police Department could boast a state-of-the-art patrol boat.

A slight fog reflects the festive street-lamps on Market Street on Christmas Eve, 1929.

RAW DEALS AND A NEW DEAL

(1930–1939)

Although the militant labor union movement had a long tradition in San Francisco, the stock market crash in 1929 and the Depression that followed finally created a critical mass of disaffected workers convinced that Capitalism was not working for them. A few Communists and anarchists would not have brought the labor battle to the streets of San Francisco if many thousands of ordinary Joes and Janes, making an average of $17 a week, hadn't marched along with them.

The pot began to simmer when the many supporters of former labor leader Thomas Mooney, convicted for the Preparedness Day Bombing in 1916, finally prevailed and managed to have his trial reviewed in 1933. It would take several years before he and his assistant, Warren K. Billings, were released—with Mooney spending 22 years in prison for a crime he did not commit. The lid hit the ceiling on July 3, 1934. It started on the San Francisco docks with striking Longshoremen and their sympathizers surging across a police cordon in several locations. After several days of acrimonious street fighting between police, strikers, and the National Guard, several strikers were dead and many injured. Sympathetic strikes multiplied until a general strike, affecting the entire Pacific Coast, finally ended on July 19, 1934. From that time on, the unions set the menu, and employers generally had to swallow their demands or be shut down by strikers. Unionization spread from the wharves to the warehouses to just about every major employer in the city. Between 1934 and the start of World War II, there was seldom a day when some union was not on strike in the city.

Although Roosevelt's New Deal helped put many men to work, many others lost their way, ending up on what photographer Dorothea Lange called "Skid Row" on Howard Street. There they panhandled and drank their best years away, hopelessly mired in addiction, petty crime, and vagrancy.

The Golden Gate International Exposition opened in 1939 on Treasure Island, a bright spot at the end of the decade. Here in the amusement park section of the fair, known as the Gayway, erotic dancer Sally Rand rounded up her girls at Sally Rand's Nude Ranch, a much-needed and barely legal distraction.

In the aftermath of the Preparedness Day Bombing in 1916, labor leader Thomas Mooney and his assistant, Warren K. Billings, had been convicted in hasty trials in a lynch-mob atmosphere. Lack of evidence had troubled President Woodrow Wilson, who commuted Mooney's death sentence to life imprisonment. Fremont Older, editor of the *News Call-Bulletin,* had taken on a new crusade to prove Mooney innocent, and he was joined by anarchists Alexander Berkman and Emma Goldman, Hollywood celebrities, and many others. In 1933, Mooney won the right to a new trial. In this photo, the Mooney family hears a trial date set for May 22, 1933. From left to right above are Belle Hammerberg (Mrs. Mooney's sister), Madeleine Wieland (Billings's cousin), Mrs. Mary Mooney (Mooney's mother), John Mooney (Mooney's brother), and Anna Mooney (Mooney's sister).

Thomas Mooney did not always act appreciatively toward those who tried to free him. According to editor Fremont Older's wife, Mooney sent unpleasant letters to her husband even as he worked for Mooney's release. "If I were imprisoned for a crime I hadn't committed," Fremont Older reasoned, "I suppose I'd be bitter too." Here Thomas Mooney talks to H. R. Hill, a *Post Enquirer* reporter at the San Francisco City Jail on May 19, 1933. Mooney was being held awaiting trial before Judge Louis Ward.

Although the Supreme Court upheld Mooney's original conviction in 1937, over the course of two decades, the evidence of perjury and false testimony presented at the original trial was overwhelming. One piece of evidence brought forth in the new trial was this photograph taken at the Preparedness Day Parade, showing Thomas Mooney on the roof (without hat) leaning out to see the procession just minutes before the bomb exploded 1.5 miles away. Governor Culbert Olson pardoned Mooney on January 7, 1939. Although he had become estranged from his former assistant Warren Billings, Mooney went to work to have him released as well, and the governor pardoned Billings in October of that year.

In the 1930s, the majority of those involved in the labor movement on the Pacific Coast were liberal Democrats. However, a much smaller group of conservatives, and an even smaller group of avowed Communists, made much noise in the press. The Depression continued with no end in sight, and the ranks of the unemployed swelled as this general protest was held in San Francisco on January 19, 1931. Meanwhile, the power of the maritime unions under the leadership of the International Longshoremen's Association continued to grow in San Francisco. On the opposing side, employers and businessmen coalesced as the Industrial Association.

On May 9, 1934, the Industrial Longshoremen's Association moved to overcome striking maritime workers by transporting goods from the piers to the warehouses. The police and unionists had their first clash on Tuesday, July 3, 1934, when police pushed strikers back several blocks from the pier and warehouse. Police on motorcycles tried to protect the trucks, while mounted officers swinging clubs waded into enraged crowds, swelled to several thousand by sympathetic union unemployed throughout the Bay Area. Fighting broke out in several locations, and police hurled tear gas bombs into crowds, as shown above. Choking with eyes streaming tears, strikers threw the smoking grenades back at the police. Strikers attacked police with rocks and bricks, overturned trucks, and fought with sticks and fists. Several of the scab truck drivers were beaten. At the end of the day, several officers and strikers had been injured.

The July 4th holiday did not cool the flames of the Longshoremen's Strike, and on Thursday, July 5, renewed rioting prompted Governor Merriam to call out the National Guard. Street fighting swept the Embarcadero and Ferry Building, deadlocking the industrial area and Rincon Hill. Before the terrifying day was over, two strikers had been killed by police bullets, and another had died from his injuries. Thirty-one people had been shot by police, and an untold number, including police, had been injured by clubs, gas, fists, stones, and bricks. Chief of Police William Quinn was enraged by the governor's call for the National Guard. The scene above, although undated, was probably taken during the confusion and violence on July 5.

The worst of the fighting picked up in the afternoon after an odd, informal truce was called during the lunch hour. A group of strikers surrounded a police car and attempted to tip it over, which prompted police to fire shotguns in the air. One of the policemen fired into the crowd, killing a striking seaman, Howard Sperry, and wounding a strike sympathizer, shown here in front of the International Longshoremen's Association headquarters at 113 Steuart Street. Within an hour, two other men had died, one from gunshot wounds, and the other from the effects of a tear gas bomb that struck him in the head.

Outraged over the events of Bloody Thursday, July 5, 1934, teamsters in both San Francisco and Oakland voted to strike. On Sunday, July 8, the entire downtown area was taken over by a crowd of 40,000 silent, peaceful mourners during a funeral for the slain strikers. After dozens of Bay Area unions voted to strike over the next few days, the San Francisco Labor Council voted on July 14 to call a general strike. The strike lasted four days, July 16 through July 19, and shut down most Pacific ports. Truck drivers joined the first day. While food deliveries continued with the permission of the strike committee, many small businesses closed, posting signs in support of the strikers. Even movie theaters and nightclubs shut down. This scene records continuing street melees in San Francisco on July 6, 1934.

On July 17, 1934, the National Guard, the SFPD, and armed vigilantes (said to be agents of the employer's Industrial Union) attacked the Marine Workers' Industrial Union headquarters, the ILA soup kitchen, and the Workers' Ex-Servicemen's League headquarters, arresting 150 and destroying the latter structure. More raids were carried out at the Workers' Open Forum and the Western Worker Building opposite City Hall that contained a bookstore and the main offices of the Communist Party, shown above. It was also destroyed, as were several other facilities. An ACLU lawyer was kidnapped and beaten, while vigilantes seized 13 radicals in San Jose and turned them over to the sheriff of an adjoining county. In Hayward, someone erected a scaffold in front of City Hall with a noose and a sign reading "Reds beware." Both sides eventually claimed victory, but the International Longshoremen's Union was officially entrenched by arbitration on October 12, 1934.

Around 1939, photographer Dorothea Lange captured these men drinking during daylight hours in an area of San Francisco that she called "Skid Row" on Howard Street, one of her favorite scenic locations. There she recorded men beyond the reach of a New Deal, panhandling and drinking their days away, hopelessly mired in addiction, petty crime, and vagrancy.

Following Spread: With the repeal of Prohibition in 1933, bars and dance halls reopened on Pacific Street. Although the gin and sin mills would never achieve the infamy they once enjoyed before Red Light District abatement in 1917, they became popular nightspots along with many others around the city. Prohibition had the unexpected effect of drawing many respectable young women to the speakeasies, and these former flappers continued to frequent San Francisco nightclubs and bars, now somewhat chastened and defanged.

In 1931, Agostino Giutoli opened the 365 Club on Market Street with partner Monk Young. Giutoli had arrived a couple of years before with $2 in his pocket, working first as a janitor, then a bus boy, and finally a cook at the Palace Hotel. Because his new partner could not pronounce his name, Agostino settled for the nickname "Bimbo," Italian for "boy." The club quickly became one of the most popular nightclubs on the West Coast, partly due to the showgirl cabarets, one of which featured a young Rita Cansino (later Rita Hayworth) and of course, "Dolfina, the Girl in a Fishbowl," seen here around 1939. Mirrors create the illusion of a nude swimmer frolicking with the goldfish in the tank behind the bar, but the girl really lounges in a room below. Bimbo's moved to 1025 Columbus Avenue in 1951, but Dolfina came along and continues to be an attraction.

Sally Rand, born Harriet Helen Gould Beck in Missouri in 1904, began her remarkable stage career as Billie Beck, a burlesque dancer noted for her ostrich feather fan dance and her balloon bubble dance. She also acted on stage and in silent films, given the name Sally Rand by director Cecil B. DeMille. Rand became a star at the 1933 Chicago World's Fair, where she was arrested four times in a single day for indecent exposure while riding a horse down Chicago streets. The nudity was allegedly illusory. Three years later, she landed in San Francisco, opening the Music Box burlesque house, where she reprised her famous dances. The Music Box later became the Great American Music Hall.

Following Spread: This skyline of San Francisco looks northeast from Douglas Street near 28th Street.

Dancer Sally Rand had shaken quite a tail feather at the California Pacific International Exposition in San Diego in 1936, and when the eyes of the world turned to San Francisco during the Golden Gate International Exposition in 1939, Sally was there. By this time, she had a few hired hands to help with the chores at Sally Rand's Nude Ranch, which opened with the fair on Treasure Island. Here one of the girls is ready to giddy-up, while another rounds up the bewildered sheep.

THE WAR AT HOME

(1940–1949)

Only patriotism and a world war could divert the surge of power wielded by the new striking unions. The continuous, multi-faceted fight for better wages, a shorter work week, and better working conditions throughout the Bay Area ground to a temporary halt as the country mobilized and the longshoremen, machinists, and just about everyone else over 18 years old enlisted or rolled up their sleeves. The workplace would never be the same again, and large numbers of women and blacks would eventually win places in the unions that had been the bastion of white males.

Just as overt discrimination against the Chinese in San Francisco was finally drawing to a close after almost a century, bigotry reared up again, impacting the lives of at least 110,000 Japanese Americans living in the West. In the months following the Pearl Harbor attack on December 7, 1941, growing paranoia and an insidious racism blended into a toxic brew, Order No. 9066, giving military commanders the authority to remove all persons of Japanese ancestry from the Pacific Coast. For the first time in the history of the country, United States citizens, many with sons serving in the military, were stripped of their rights, rounded up, and taken to assembly centers and internment camps. It had become a crime to be of Japanese ancestry. Scrambling to rent or sell their property and belongings, usually at a great loss, some families were incarcerated for almost three years. Even progressive liberals like President Franklin Roosevelt and then–State Attorney General Earl G. Warren (later U.S. chief justice) recommended and executed the order. Only one politician spoke out publicly against it, Colorado Governor Ralph Lawrence Carr, who then lost his bid for re-election.

Alcatraz Island, converted from a military prison to a maximum-security federal penitentiary in 1934, housed some of the most hardened criminals in the country by the late 1940s. Of the 14 escape attempts from "the Rock" from 1934 to its closing in 1965, none was more dramatic than the three-day uprising by six prisoners who managed to take over a cellblock on May 2, 1946. Like battles named in the recent global war, this riot became known as the "Battle of Alcatraz."

The 1934 maritime general strike emboldened workers and solidified the power of the International Longshoremen's Association. Union organizers moved off the dock and onto the warehouses, where workers made as little as 50 cents an hour. If the employer did not negotiate, they would go on strike. The union bug spread from the warehouses to Safeway, department stores, utilities, and hotels. From 1934 to 1940, there was hardly a day when some strike was not in progress. By 1940, the West Coast maritime workers had split from International Longshoremen's Association (ILA) and formed their own new union, the International Longshore and Warehouse Union (ILWU). Violence would erupt again in May 1940, when mounted San Francisco police officers, shown here, escorted strikebreakers at the Euclid Candy Company.

The SFPD continued to protect employers' interests, citing Communist infiltration of the unions as justification, just as they had during the 1934 strike. On March 8, 1940, police officers beat and arrested ILWU pickets, including some women, during a strike at the Euclid Candy Company. In this photograph, John A. Gomez, 29, has collapsed in the gutter one hour after a morning battle with police, when he received a blow to his head. He returned later to the picket line and was arrested. The fact that police and union workers often shared ethnic, class, and religious backgrounds did not ameliorate the antagonism between them.

In 1922, Australian seaman Harry Bridges came ashore to work as a San Francisco longshoreman at age 19. Inspired by socialist author Jack London, Harry became a leader in the ILU and the ILWU. As employers and police battled the perceived Communist influence in local unions, Harry became a prime target. This photograph catches one scene in a long legal battle that spanned three decades, the government's second attempt to deport Bridges as an undesirable alien. Here on April 1, 1941, he is going into a second day of hearings. At left, heads showing just above the prosecution table are Albert del Guercio of the Los Angeles immigration office and Paul V. Myron, special assistant to the U.S. attorney general. On the other side of the prosecution table are Judge Charles Charles N. Goodwin from Washington, D.C., chief attorney for the prosecution, and Trent Doser, an immigration inspector from San Pedro. At the defense table at right is Harry Bridges facing his three attorneys: Richard Gladstein, Carol King, chief counsel, and Aubrey Grossman.

A line of spectators waits to get in to see the second deportation trial of Harry Bridges on March 31, 1941. Although Harry Bridges' conviction was reversed by the Supreme Court in 1945, the federal government prosecuted Bridges in 1948 for perjury for stating on his naturalization papers that he was not a member of the Communist Party. He was convicted again, and once more the case was brought before the Supreme Court, which overturned the second conviction in 1953. The government then proceeded with a civil case to revoke Bridges' naturalization. The last judge finally ruled in Harry's favor in 1954, and the government did not appeal. Harry Bridges remained president of the ILWU until his retirement in 1977, leading the organization through many changes, including mechanization of the docks and inclusion of blacks and women in the union.

World War II would mobilize the country, and the era of continuous strikes by unionized workers would abate, calmed by a salve of patriotism. No other industry was more crucial to the successful war effort than shipbuilding. Shown here on June 4, 1941, shipbuilders return to work through a picket line of striking machinists at Bethlehem Steel in San Francisco. Between 3,000 and 3,500 workers heeded the back-to-work order issued by AFL Metal Trades Council. The pickets, members of the striking AFL Machinists Union, Local 68, watched silently as they saw the tide turn. The return to work was a command by the National Defense Mediation Board, pending a Washington, D.C., hearing.

The threat of Communism diminished temporarily during the buildup to World War II, as the Soviet Union became an uneasy ally in the battle to fight a greater evil. The SFPD now had to focus on more immediate dangers. In this photo taken on July 16, 1941, "G-men," agents from the Federal Bureau of Investigation, instruct local police on methods used by saboteurs.

Japanese immigrants had been targeted for labor issues since at least 1910, but after the attack on Pearl Harbor, racial paranoia reigned. General John L. DeWitt, stationed at the Presidio, warned of "a violent outburst of coordinated and controlled sabotage." DeWitt; Admiral John W. Greenslade, commander of the Navy's 12th District; Attorney General Earl Warren (later governor and U.S. chief justice); and L.A. Mayor Fletcher Bowron were among the instigators of the order. By the time this photograph was taken on February 21, 1942, many San Franciscans of Japanese ancestry were voluntarily leaving their homes, or being rounded up in raids. Here Genzo Nakhiro, carrying a Bible, is escorted from his Webster Street bakery, while his wife watches in tears. At far-right is an FBI agent.

In January 1942, the Japanese in San Francisco were ordered to turn in radios and cameras, and on February 19, President Roosevelt signed Executive Order No. 9066, giving military commanders authority to remove persons of Japanese ancestry from the Pacific Coast. General DeWitt issued a voluntary evacuation order on March 2 and a mandatory order on March 27. The order would eventually result in the relocation of 110,000 people of Japanese descent, two-thirds of whom were American citizens, and some with relatives serving in the military. Most were sent to remote areas between the Sierra Nevada and Rocky Mountains. Photographer Dorothea Lange recorded this sign at 13th and Franklin streets erected by a Japanese-American storeowner, a U.S. citizen and UC Berkeley graduate, the day after Pearl Harbor. It did not save him from evacuation. According to author William Wong, he was forced to sell this store to four Chinese families.

As hundreds of "enemy aliens" were arrested in San Francisco and the San Joaquin Valley, Japanese Americans had to sell or rent all of their property and belongings, or store them in government facilities that later reported much loss and damage. The Japanese evacuation order spread to Los Angeles on May 3, 1942. By May 20, only six seriously ill Japanese remained in San Francisco hospitals. This Dorothea Lange photo from April 6, 1942, shows Japanese Americans waiting to be transported from the control station at 1701 Van Ness Avenue to an assembly center.

Local newspapers photographed Japanese students attending "high school" at the Tanforan relocation facility on April 28, 1942. Eventually, most children at Tanforan were allowed to attend other schools in the city—if they could find one that would accept them. Fearing the loss of agricultural workers, California Governor Culbert Olson had been reluctant to recommend the evacuation order in 1942. His fears were soon realized in May when it became necessary to recruit 1,500 women to harvest the crops at the standard $4 to $8 per day. Many believe that part of the motivation for interning the Japanese was to disenfranchise Japanese landowners and farmers who had been multiplying in the Central and San Joaquin valleys.

Named by Spanish explorer Juan Manuel de Ayala in 1775 for its only inhabitants, pelicans, Alcatraz Island was for many years inaccessible to the general public. By 1854, the U.S. Army Corps of Engineers built the Pacific Coast's first military fortifications and the first operating lighthouse on the Pacific Coast. Mightily armed for the Civil War, Alcatraz boasted cannons and massive Rodman guns capable of sinking ships three miles away. The prison would fire only one 400-pound cannon during its military history, missing its target, an unidentified ship. Alcatraz began receiving military prisoners in 1861, and by 1920, a three-story cell house was fully occupied. This view of Alcatraz was taken in 1954, after its conversion to a federal penitentiary.

Although inmates at the military prison on Alcatraz were usually convicted of desertion or lesser crimes, discipline included strict rules of silence, and prisoners could remain in their cells only to sleep. Additional punishment meant solitary confinement, ball-and-ankle chains, and bread-and-water diets. Favored inmates acted as servants to the resident families, as did a community of Chinese house servants who formed the largest civilian community on the island. Most inmates who tried to escape turned back in the freezing waters and had to be rescued. This is the interior of a federal prison cell in 1939.

In 1934, Alcatraz was taken over by the Department of Justice and converted into a grim maximum-security penitentiary to house some of the nation's most hardened criminals. At that time, Robert Burge redesigned the facility to be "escape-proof." This narrow recreation yard, shown here on April 19, 1941, offered the only sunshine an inmate could hope for amid the fog and wind of the San Francisco Bay. Although several well-known criminals, such as Al Capone, George "Machine-Gun" Kelly, Alvin Karpis (the first "Public Enemy Number One"), Arthur "Doc" Barker, and Robert Stroud (the "Birdman of Alcatraz") did time on the Rock, the majority of Alcatraz inmates were not famous.

During its transformation into a maximum-security federal prison, Alcatraz cell houses were modernized with electricity, tool-proof bars, and iron window coverings. Utility tunnels were cemented to prevent access. Each cell house had about 600 cells, all arranged in the center so that none touched an exterior wall. Escape from a cell required an inmate to enter a breezeway overlooked by elevated gun galleries behind iron rod barriers. These galleries, which contained prison keys, allowed guards to control all perimeters. This is a standard prison cell photographed on September 3, 1941.

Henry Young murdered fellow convict Rufus McCain in the aftermath of an escape attempt. On January 13, 1939, Arthur "Doc" Barker, Dale Stamphill, William Martin, Henry Young, and Rufus McCain escaped from an isolation unit by sawing through the flat iron cell bars and bending tool-proof bars on a window. They made their way down to the water's edge on the western side of the island, the path indicated here at right by a dotted line. Initially the fog was so thick that guards in the tower could not see the escapees, but Martin, Young, and McCain finally surrendered. Barker and Stamphill were shot and died when they refused to give themselves up. Months later, in December 1940, Young stabbed and killed McCain in the industries building. This photo, taken February 2, 1939, shows guarded prisoners (indicated by a circle) being marched from one of the workshops to the cellblocks.

On May 2, 1946, the most famous of all escape attempts from Alcatraz began when six prisoners overpowered guards to gain access to an elevated gun gallery where keys were kept. Achieving their first target, the key they found would not unlock the door that lead to the recreation yard—and freedom. Prison officials soon discovered the break, but Bernard Coy, Joe Cretzer, Marvin Hubbard, Sam Shockley, Miran Thompson, and Clarence Carnes continued to fight, now hopelessly trapped in the cellblock. This view shows smoke from grenades tossed through an opening in the cellblock roof, the only access point available to officials on May 4, 1946.

Remembered for years as the "Battle of Alcatraz," the famous escape attempt that began on May 2, 1946, riveted Bay Area residents for three long days. The Marines were finally called in to end the prisoner uprising. A Coast Guard patrol craft (right) can be seen in this photograph, followed by Warden James Johnston aboard the prison patrol boat, as they circle Alcatraz on May 3, the second day of the siege. The historic lighthouse and residences can be seen at upper-left, and the older military structures on the lower tier of the island. The cell houses can be seen at right and on the hilltop at center, where the battle raged.

At some point during the Alcatraz Prison standoff in May 1946, Joe Cretzer shot the officers who had been taken hostage. One of the officers, William Miller, died from his injuries. Later it was charged that Sam Shockley and Miran Thompson encouraged Cretzer to kill the guards. As the stalemate dragged on, Shockley, Thompson, and Carnes returned to their cells defeated to await the inevitable. On May 4, law enforcement officials gained entry, discovering the bodies of Bernard Coy, Cretzer, and Marvin Hubbard, presumably killed during the siege. Over the course of the three-day battle, spectators on the mainland could hear frequent explosions and see the smoke from bursting grenades. Private J. J. Weber, one of the onlookers shown here, brought a 33-power telescope along on May 4 to watch the excitement from the Municipal Fishing Pier at the foot of Van Ness Avenue; he soon went into business, charging a dime for each look in the scope.

Sam Shockley, Miran Thompson, and Clarence Carnes stood trial for the deaths of two officers during the 1946 prison uprising on Alcatraz. Shockley and Thompson were executed in the gas chamber at San Quentin in December 1948. Their executions ignited a local movement to abolish capital punishment. Carnes, age 19, received a second life sentence. Although Alcatraz was billed as escape proof, over its 29-year history as a federal prison, 36 men made 14 separate escape attempts to disprove the claim, and two men tried twice. Of these, 23 were captured, six died by bullets while escaping, and two drowned in the bay. Five men were never found, listed as "missing and presumed drowned." On the order of Attorney General Robert F. Kennedy, the prison closed on March 21, 1965.

Since the 1926 rampage of murderous, heroin-fueled Clarence "Buck" Kelly, illegal drugs played an increasing role in San Francisco crime. On the night of May 12, 1948, gunmen took two families hostage at 100 Rae Avenue, the home of Phil Baitlin (shown above). Baitlin was the general manager of two drugstores, and the thieves hoped to force him to retrieve money and narcotics while they held the families at the residence. When police officers showed up the next morning to investigate, the gunmen shot two officers, one as he stood in front of the patrol car shown in the photo. The gunmen then fled. Less than 12 hours from the time the officers were shot, police rounded up the suspects for questioning. Baitlin was able to identify all of the gunmen from a lineup.

FAMILY MATTERS AND THE END OF AN ERA

(1950–1960)

At mid-century families became the focus for many returning G.I.s, and several of the real-life crime dramas of that era involved families under stress. In a landmark case in 1953, attorneys for Russian-Armenian concentration camp survivor Lewon Melkonian argued that he shot his 60-year old wife and their boarder in a highly confused and paranoid state, essentially a temporary insanity plea. In an unusual case the same year, a grand jury refused to even indict Carolyn O'Malley, who freely admitted that she shot her husband, a highway patrolman, with his own gun. A victim of repeated abuse, she believed her act was justified for her own defense, and even her in-laws supported her claim. When Maurice Moskovitz, son of Rochester Big & Tall men's clothing storeowner, was kidnapped for a $500,000 ransom in 1954, police used telephone tracing to break the case. In 1955, a newborn baby disappeared from the nursery at Mt. Zion hospital, prompting the largest door-to-door search in the city's history. Adding to the drama, which dragged on for nine days, was the fact that the baby was Jewish, and the young mother a fugitive from the Nazis who had lost her family to Hitler's ovens. That case was finally solved not by technology, but by alert law enforcement officers.

Mid-century was also a pivotal era for public reexamination of two issues associated with places that lie at San Francisco's doorstep: the gas chamber at San Quentin, and the Golden Gate Bridge. The execution of convicted robber and rapist Caryl Chessman on December 8, 1955, was not the first case to ignite controversy over capital punishment, but it set a precedent for organized protests that continues to this day. By the 1950s, the Golden Gate Bridge had become a visual symbol of San Francisco, but it had also become apparent that this celebrated span was the most popular suicide site in the nation, perhaps the world. There is no accurate tally of those who have stepped over its four-foot rail, but estimates put the figure at about 1,500, some of whom traveled long distances to reach the bridge. The issues plaguing this era prompted the question: What is the role of law enforcement for those who choose to take their own lives, and should the life of another be taken for any reason other than self-defense?

Criminologist Francis X. Latulipe, Jr., is shown here on July 25, 1950, working in a corner of his new $100,000 laboratory in the "penthouse" of the Hall of Justice at Washington and Kearny streets. At right is a ballistics comparison microscope that can be used to trace a bullet to the gun that fired it. Other devices are used for magnifying and evaluating evidence. Inspector Latulipe was the first criminologist in the department, and he was called the nation's foremost authority on fingerprints and handwriting analysis, serving as an expert witness in many criminal trials throughout the state. He died in 1959.

By 1950, fingerprints were routinely collected at every crime scene, to be processed at the crime lab by SFPD criminologist Inspector Francis X. Latulipe. Shown here are SFPD officers Pat Walsh (left) and Leonard Wiebe dusting for fingerprints at 1606 Sacramento Street in the basement apartment of Mary McIntyre, 25, who was "slugged" by an intruder after returning from a dance in Fairfax in Marin County on June 6, 1950.

San Francisco Police Department criminologist Inspector Francis X. Latulipe, Jr., also worked outside his $100,000 crime lab. Here, on February 16, 1953, Latulipe attempts to determine if a crime has been committed by examining a bathtub in which a body had been found floating facedown.

In this photograph, confessed murderer Roman Rodriguez reenacts his crime for investigators in Dolores Park on March 25, 1952. Rodriguez claimed that he approached 16-year-old Hilda Rosa Pagan, and that the pair sat atop the terrace (left) before going down to the lawn area, where they embraced. Here Rodriguez beat the girl with his fists and left her unconscious. Her battered body was found in a hole in the shrubbery. The trial jury would visit the same location in July before convicting Rodriguez of murder.

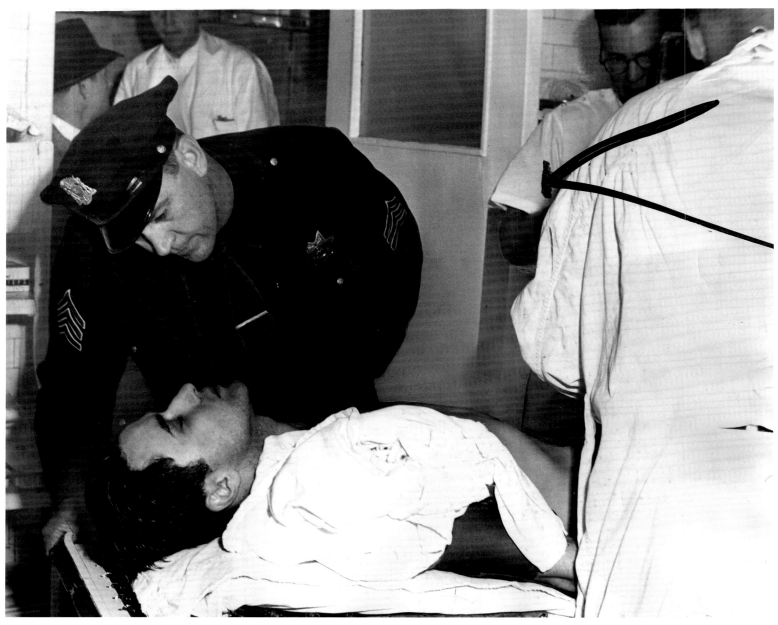

Guns in the house and an approaching holiday may have played a role in this attempted suicide on December 23, 1953. SFPD Sergeant Kenneth Carstensen offers support to fellow police officer Harold E. Cole, 24, just before he undergoes surgery for a bullet wound in the abdomen at Mission Emergency Hospital. Cole shot himself following a quarrel with his estranged wife. One study in the San Francisco's coroner's records tallied reported suicides between July 1956 and June 1964. Of the 1,664 suicides reported, the most common method was ingestion of toxic substances. This finding significantly deviated from national statistics, which listed firearms as the most common method. Researchers attributed the difference to more conscientious postmortem toxicology studies in San Francisco, speculating that many suicides by ingestion went unreported in other parts of the nation.

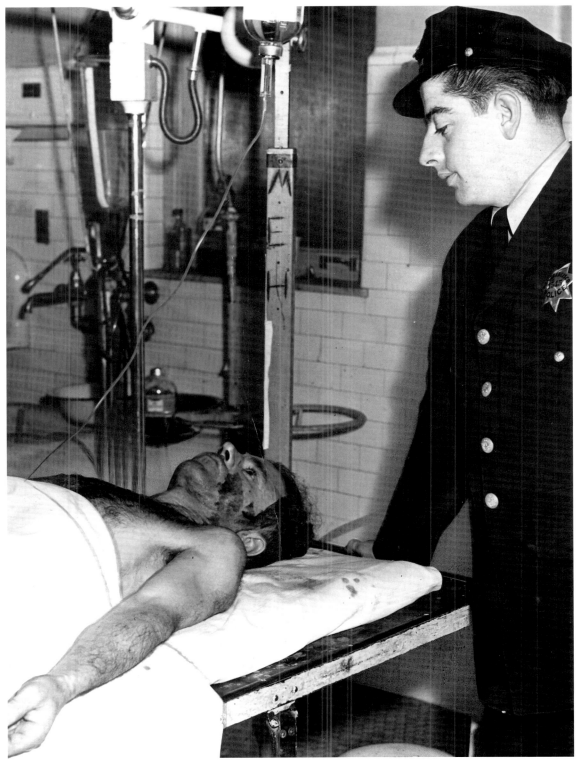

SFPD officer Thomas Smith stands over Lewon Melkonian, a Russian-Armenian refugee and concentration camp survivor, who murdered his 60-year-old wife, Goharik, and their boarder, and then tried to take his own life on January 24, 1953. His trial became a landmark case. Melkonian, in a highly confused, paranoid state, believed that his wife was romantically involved with the boarder, Lewon Usunian, and that they planned to poison him. Although Melkonian took the stand and freely admitted his crime, his defense was not based on a plea of insanity. Expert psychiatric testimony was used to prove that because of his mental illness, he did not possess malice aforethought, a defense now commonly referred to as temporary insanity. Although never delusional, Melkonian showed severe anxiety and depression, which convinced the jury. He was convicted of manslaughter and given two consecutive prison terms.

Completed in 1937 and burnished reddish-orange (not gold) with countless layers of Rust-o-leum paint, the Golden Gate Bridge is reputed to be the most popular suicide site in the United States and perhaps the world. Because many acts of suicide—or homicide—from the bridge are not witnessed, there is no accurate count of those who have made the plunge. Some take taxis to the site, and police have found abandoned rental cars in the parking lot. The strong current might well take a body out to sea without any witnesses. It has been reported that new suicides from the bridge average one every two weeks. This heavenly view of the 4,200-foot span was captured on July 28, 1954.

From the deck of the Golden Gate Bridge, there is a 245-foot drop to the frigid waters below. It takes approximately four seconds for an object approaching 86 miles per hour to hit the water. Those not fatally broken by the impact soon succumb to drowning or hypothermia. Bridge designer Joseph Strauss was just five feet tall, so he made the bridge railing four feet high, low enough for anyone to clear in an ill-considered heartbeat. This view faces north from the San Francisco shore.

Perhaps the first to step over the rail of the Golden Gate Bridge, ready for a new frontier, was World War I veteran Harold Wobber in August 1937. Wobber paused at the rail, looked at a stranger, said "This is as far as I go," and jumped to his death. Only 26 people are known to have survived the leap. Miraculously, one young man not only survived, but swam to shore and drove himself to the hospital in 1979. In this photo, *Santa Rosa Press Democrat* photographer John LeBaron tells highway patrolman Theodore McGuire how he tried unsuccessfully to keep a young man from jumping off the Golden Gate Bridge on August 22, 1952.

By the time this night scene was captured in Chinatown in 1955, the tong wars, slave girls, and opium dens were a thing of the distant past. A little illegal gambling continued discreetly and the usual suspects still hung out in the alleys, but Chinatown and its famous nightclubs were now safe for tourists.

Carolyn O'Malley, shown second from right on January 6, 1953, fatally shot her husband John, a California highway patrolman, during an argument about how to raise 10 chinchillas in their Sunset District home. Carolyn, shown here flanked by her attorney, James McInnes, and a police matron, testified that her husband threatened to kill her for putting two chinchillas in the same cage. When John O'Malley returned later on New Year's Eve, he resumed his threats, so Carolyn shot him with his .38 revolver. Afterward, she wandered outside to tell a neighbor, who immediately called John O'Malley, Sr., and his wife Irene, who lived close by. After hearing testimony from all concerned, including Carolyn's four young children, a grand jury refused to indict the slight, 34-year-old housewife. She was cared for by the parents of the man she killed. Reportedly, O'Malley, Jr., was once a good husband and father but began to regularly beat and threaten his wife.

This mundane telephone booth at San Francisco's West Portal Avenue and Sloat Boulevard was a key element in cracking a famous kidnapping case that was remarkable for two reasons. First, it was an early case of tracing a telephone call to its source, and second, it may have been the only time that the SFPD managed to maintain a press blackout for four days about a sensational crime, the January 15, 1954, kidnapping of Leonard Moskovitz, son of Maurice Moskovitz, who owned Rochester Big & Tall men's clothing store. Kidnappers forced Leonard to write a ransom note asking for $500,000, but when one of them placed a telephone call to Leonard's twin brother, Alfred, on January 19, he was able to keep the kidnapper on the line long enough for police to trace the call and drag Joseph Lear from this phone booth at 2:45 A.M. Lear led police back to the kidnappers' lair, where Leonard Moskovitz, who lived to be 90, was found unharmed.

When newspapers reported on September 20, 1955, that a newborn baby had been kidnapped from Mt. Zion Hospital, the public was transfixed. Over the course of the next 10 days, up to one-third of the entire SFPD was mobilized to find the child and the overweight blond female who was suspected of snatching him. The kidnapped baby was Jewish, the son of Dr. Sanford Marcus, resident physician at Mt. Zion, and pretty, young Hanna Eichenwald Marcus, a survivor of the Holocaust whose family had been incinerated in Hitler's ovens. Here Police Lieutenant Ed Farrell briefs officers at the Southern Station on September 21 for a door-to-door search that would eventually reach 260,000 homes.

Dr. Sanford Marcus taped a plea to kidnappers that was played on radio stations, and the press hounded the couple to record their anguish. Hanna Marcus was so prostrate that doctors feared for her life. Police, as shown above on September 21, fielded hundreds of calls and many hoaxes. As Hanna began to recover and returned home from the hospital, 27-year-old Betty Jean Benedicto of Stockton, described by the *Examiner* as "blond, blowsy, and blubbering," finally returned the unharmed baby on September 29, but only after she had been spotted and questioned by eagle-eyed Stockton Deputy Sheriff Osvaldo Vanucci. Benedicto had faked a pregnancy to please her new 52-year-old husband, and stole the child because the name Marcus was similar to her husband's first name, Mark. After a highly publicized trial full of histrionics and comments from *Chronicle* columnist Herb Caen, Benedicto was judged insane and remanded to Mendocino State Hospital.

Like the execution of "Battle of Alcatraz" leader Sam Shockley in December 1948, serial robber and rapist Caryl Chessman, convicted that same year, reignited the capital punishment controversy. Chessman was sentenced to death under the "Little Lindbergh Law" because his crimes included kidnapping and transporting his victims, dragging them a few feet, in order to rape them. He first attracted public attention by acting as his own attorney, regaling the jury with a rambling defense that alternately claimed he was the victim of mistaken identity, a frame-up, and police torture to extract a confession. During a decade on death row, his appeals deflected eight execution dates. In this photo taken on December 8, 1955, Chessman is being led into the post office building to make another appeal for a stay of execution. He is flanked by San Quentin guards J. R. Thomas (left) and Lieutenant L. J. Morin.

The Hall of Justice, rebuilt on the southeast corner of Washington and Kearny streets after the earthquake and fire of 1906, had become the object of many complaints by mid-century. Police and court officials griped about small, cramped offices and antiquated plumbing. One area of concern was the city jail, shown in this photograph on May 25, 1956. The narrow corridor also served as a dining room and recreation area. The state of California added its voice to the chorus of critics by condemning the building.

This real-life standoff outside the Old Poodle Dog Restaurant on Post Street on July 14, 1957, recalled the dramas San Franciscans watched on their new television sets. On a quiet Sunday evening, four gunmen took 12 hostages inside the famous eatery, as police, shown here, massed outside with guns drawn. Among the hostages were the wife of Federal Judge George B. Harris, restaurant owners Mr. and Mrs. Louis Lalanne, and a family with three children. One waiter was able to slip out the freight elevator in the basement and alert police. As SFPD officers spoke to them over a loudspeaker, the gunmen panicked, realizing that all exits had been secured. Desperate, the four men managed to heave themselves through a narrow skylight. They got away with $160, but in their haste forgot to grab the $920 they had taken from the cash register and safe. The entire episode lasted about 30 minutes, just like the TV shows—but without the commercials.

The famous decade of public protest and riots in the Bay Area in the 1960s was actually preceded by a few wild public melees like the one seen here in July 1958 at Kezar Stadium. At issue here was a fence at the east end of the stadium that blocked the fans' view of a 49er football game, and the crowd made their displeasure known. The Parks and Recreation Department put up the fence to keep the general admission ticket holders from drifting into reserved seating. Two years before, in September 1956, a teenage knife and fistfight precipitated a riot that required police to round up the miscreants. Ten boys were injured and 250 policemen converged on the stadium.

Once again the crowd turned into a mob at Kezar Stadium on December 15, 1958, following a football game between the 49ers and the Baltimore Colts. The fact that the 49ers won by a score of 21–12 in their final game of the season seemed a good enough reason to celebrate with a fight resulting in bloody noses, shattered windshields, and a pitched battle between over 80 policemen and 300 young fans. At one point the rioters overwhelmed police to remove two prisoners from a paddy wagon on the field, shown here. The beleaguered police succeeded in arresting only one unlucky demonstrator. By 1958, protest seemed to be in the air.

Looking neat and businesslike, pickets from the Northern California Committees for the Abolition of Nuclear Weapons demonstrate in front of San Francisco Civic Auditorium on October 21, 1958. They were here to protest the visit of President Dwight D. Eisenhower, who was addressing a public rally inside the building. Some carry signs that read "No More Quemoys!" This refers to an incident earlier in the year on an island group west of Taiwan that had led to the deployment of the U.S. 7th Fleet. Fortunately, an escalation of hostilities with the Chinese was avoided. President Eisenhower entered the building by a back door, avoiding the pickets.

Resentment over the activities of the House un-American Activities Subcommittee erupted on Friday, May 13, 1960. The Committee had subpoenaed 110 public school teachers in early June 1959 because of possible Communist affiliations or activities. Ten months later, these hearings in the supervisors chamber of City Hall, would result in four of those teachers leaving the school system. Several moribund student groups from local campuses suddenly revived and joined forces to protest, first gathering a crowd of about 700 at Union Square the previous day. On Friday, several hundred demonstrators milled outside City Hall, while a crowd of about 200 protesters made it into the building where they were sitting on the floor singing.

On May 13, 1960, a crowd of 200 demonstrators sat and sang in the hallways outside the supervisors chambers at City Hall where the House un-American Activities Subcommittee hearings were proceeding. For no known cause, one policeman turned a fire hose on the crowd inside, causing some to run, but most to stay, angry and wet. At the end of the day, many protesters were injured, and 68 were arrested. Here a helmeted policeman puts a student protestor in a headlock while another policeman comes to the officer's aid with a billyclub. Note the wet clothing.

When the House un-American Activities Subcommittee sessions at City Hall resumed on Saturday, May 14, about 1,500 protesters and a larger crowd of sympathetic spectators showed up. Perhaps anticipating the chaos and bloodshed of the 1934 Longshoremen's Strike, Police Chief Thomas Cahill took no chances. Assuming personal command of the operation, he directed a hand-picked squad that included 13 veteran mounted policemen transported from Golden Gate Park, 56 uniformed and 25 plainclothes policemen, FBI agents, and army intelligence officers. Three patrol wagons stood by and the fire department pumping engines were ready to move in with high-pressure hoses. This photograph shows the police and demonstrators on the steps of City Hall on May 13 or 14, 1960.

An era was ending in San Francisco, and with it some of the city's most familiar icons. SFPD Sergeant John J. Manion, the template for the hardboiled police detective and perhaps the real life inspiration for Dashiell Hammett's Sam Spade in *The Maltese Falcon,* died in March of 1959. Manion was the boyhood friend of Police Chief Daniel O'Brien, and because of Manion's successful abatement of the "Black Hand," or Mafia, in North Beach, O'Brien tapped him to take over the Chinatown Squad in 1921. According to author Lani Ah Tye Farkas, Manion was confronted by two tong murders on his first day at work, but soon arrested and convicted two men for those murders. One was executed and one died in San Quentin, so it was clear that Manion meant business. Hammett also lived in San Francisco during that era, a former Pinkerton detective who admired Manion's exploits. Although his tactics may have been rough and possibly illegal, Jack Manion got the job done, eliminating all slave girls, and most opium, gambling, and tong warfare in Chinatown. The last tong murder recorded was in 1926. Manion won the respect of Chinatown because he respected the Chinese, who demanded that "Sargey" stay on until his retirement in 1949. Dashiell Hammett died January 10, 1961, never having created a more compelling character than Sam Spade.

Few bemoaned the passing of the old Hall of Justice at Kearny and Washington streets when it was razed in 1961. It had been condemned for several years, and all looked forward to a new modern facility, just as San Franciscans looked forward to a new progressive era and the race for space. It would also be a new era of crime detection and police facilities. Never again would anyone be able to report, as they did just before it was demolished on May 18, 1961, that the front doors of the Hall of Justice had never once been locked.

NOTES ON THE PHOTOGRAPHS

These notes, listed by page number, attempt to include all aspects known of the photographs. Each of the photographs is identified by the page number, photograph's title or description, photographer and collection, archive, and call or box number when applicable. Although every attempt was made to collect available data, in some cases complete data was unavailable due to the age and condition of some of the photographs and records.